PRAISE FOR *STRENGTH-BASED LEADERSHIP COACHING IN ORGANIZATIONS*

D1522616

'This groundbreaking book provides a comprehensive and insightful discourse on strength-based leadership coaching in organizations. This is a tour de force on this important and contemporary subject.' **Professor Stephen Palmer, President, International Society for Coaching Psychology**

'My frustration over the years with buying and participating in leadership development programmes is not knowing which bits really work. Dr Doug MacKie combines his skill of being a first-rate leadership coach with a research-rich approach to cut through to what really matters. This book is equally applicable to practitioners as it is to leaders who want to practically understand what they can do to improve organizational performance.' **Guy Templeton, President and CEO, Asia Pacific, WSP | Parsons Brinckerhoff**

'This is a book that needed to be written. It not only nails down the lid on the coffin of deficit-based leadership development, but provides a pragmatic and practical agenda for moving to a strength-based approach at both individual and corporate level. A must-read for anyone serious about building the capacity of existing and future leaders to manage in a complex and dynamic environment.' **Professor David Clutterbuck, David Clutterbuck Partnership**

'While many executive coaches are increasingly seeing the value from using a strength-based approach in their work with leaders, *Strength-Based Leadership Coaching in Organizations* takes both the science and the application of strengths coaching to another level! Based on the latest research, this is a must-read for any practising coach, both internal and external to an organization, looking to further develop their people and teams.' **Katherine Tulpa, CEO, Association for Coaching**

'*Strength-Based Leadership Coaching in Organizations* provides a rare and timely combination of scholarly critique and pragmatic application on the topic of positive leadership development. The overview and critique of leadership development research, and strength-based approaches in particular, in the first half of the book is impressive in both its breadth and depth. The second half of the book, written for coaching psychologists, leaders and managers, and leaders of work teams, spells out clearly how to apply the concepts and theories introduced previously. The author concludes with well-considered cautionary comments and criticisms of strength-based coaching, illustrating his extensive experience as a researcher and practitioner in this space, and his credibility as the book's author. The book represents a valuable resource for both researchers and practitioners who have few similar quality alternatives to consult in terms of combination of evidence-based and applied information.' **Sandy Gordon, PhD, FAPS, Associate Professor, Sport and Exercise Psychology, The University of Western Australia, and *ICPR* Co-ordinating Editor**

'*Strength-Based Leadership Coaching in Organizations* takes on some of the key frustrations in contemporary leadership development theory and practice, such as the focus on negative traits, lack of evaluation, lack of practical application and lack of evidence-based decisions, and, instead, offers a new approach. Most of all, the book offers hope. A hope that through focusing on a proven strength-based approach, leaders may more regularly inspire others, find their passions and deliver sustainable performance outcomes. This surely must lead to more authentic and courageous leadership and help us start to shift the sometimes demoralizing fear-of-failure-based, negative and judgemental approach to leadership, cemented in place following the global financial crisis.

'The book will become an important guide for any serious professional working to develop better leadership at the individual, team and organizational levels.' **Rolf Moses, Director, People and Development, Norton Rose Fulbright, Australia**

Strength-Based Leadership Coaching in Organizations

An evidence-based guide to positive leadership development

Doug MacKie

Kogan Page

LONDON PHILADELPHIA NEW DELHI

First published in Great Britain and the United States in 2016 by Kogan Page Limited

2nd Floor, 45 Gee Street
London EC1V 3RS
United Kingdom
www.koganpage.com

1518 Walnut Street,
Suite 900
Philadelphia PA 19102
USA

4737/23 Ansari Road
Daryaganj
New Delhi 110002
India

© Dr Doug MacKie, 2016

ISBN   978 0 7494 7443 0
E-ISBN 978 0 7494 7444 7

British Library Cataloguing-in-Publication Data

A CIP record for this book is available from the British Library.

Library of Congress Cataloging-in-Publication Data

Names: MacKie, Doug, author.
Title: Strength-based leadership coaching in organizations : an evidence-based guide to
   positive leadership development / Doug MacKie.
Description: London ; Philadelphia : Kogan Page, [2016] | Includes bibliographical references and
   index. | Description based on print version record and CIP data provided by publisher; resource
   not viewed.
Identifiers: LCCN 2016005942 (print) | LCCN 2015050727 (ebook) | ISBN 9780749474447 (ebook) |
   ISBN 9780749474430 (paperback)
Subjects: LCSH: Leadership. | Executive coaching. | Executive ability. | Positive psychology. |
   Psychology, Industrial. | BISAC: BUSINESS & ECONOMICS / Leadership. | BUSINESS &
   ECONOMICS / Human Resources & Personnel Management. | PSYCHOLOGY / Industrial &
   Organizational Psychology.
Classification: LCC HD57.7 (print) | LCC HD57.7 .M3345 2016 (ebook) | DDC 658.4/092–dc23
LC record available at http://lccn.loc.gov/2016005942

Typeset by SPi Global
Print production managed by Jellyfish
Printed and bound by CPI Group (UK) Ltd, Croydon, CR0 4YY

CONTENTS

PREFACE

Leadership is omnipresent and so is the evidence of its limitations. Never has so much been spent on understanding and cultivating the elements of successful leadership and yet we continue to experience, sometimes on a daily level, the dark side of leadership behaviour. As I write this introduction, the CEO of Volkswagen has recently stepped down in the wake of the scandal around the use of software to reduce apparent diesel emissions, and the founding chairman of 7-Eleven has also resigned and the new chairman admitted that the company and its franchisees had failed vulnerable people in their workforce. Management derailment remains alarmingly high with estimates ranging from 50–70 per cent; leaders repeatedly struggle to identify their strengths and significant amounts of leadership potential are wasted due to restrictive beliefs about talent being the inherited endowment of the privileged few.

So why another book about leadership and its development? Essentially because leadership matters, and how we can develop it more effectively is a critical question in today's corporate environment. My own research on positive leadership including strength-based approaches tells me that this approach offers a significant augmentation to the traditional leadership development approaches. The positivity movement has been gaining traction since its renaissance in 2000 but has been slow to penetrate organizations. This needs to and is changing as, despite the vast amounts spent on corporate leadership development annually, much of it is delivered in a standardized training format that discounts the individual capability of the leader, their development level, their organizational context and, above all, their specific leadership strengths. No wonder the majority of these skills don't transfer to the workplace. Individualized leadership coaching is changing this paradigm and at last championing a more bespoke, strength-orientated and contextual approach to developing leaders. Finally, leadership models are changing and becoming more distributed, organizations are becoming more complex and demanding and leadership teams are becoming the primary source of delivery. All these factors support and require a more distributed, strength-based, developmental and collaborative approach to leadership.

However, it is early days in the strength-based approach to leadership, and some of the claims made can border on the evangelical, so remaining evidence-based is key. A core motivation for writing this book was to summarize and contribute to that evidence base so those in HR, consulting and management can make better evidence-based decisions on how to develop their leaders. The good news for those interested in this approach is that the current evidence is very encouraging: strength-based approaches do seem to augment traditional leadership development approaches offering something significantly above and beyond the traditional deficit methods.

And yet this book is also about balance and acknowledging the downside of any approach. There is a risk with strength-based approaches, inexpertly applied, that they collude with the hubris and excessive positivity sometimes found at the top of organizations. Addressing these concerns is fundamental to advancing the strength-based paradigm. That is why I review not only the evidence base for strength approaches but also the challenges and criticisms of the model.

What's in the book?

Each chapter in the book is designed to be read in relative isolation with references included by chapter rather than combined at the end. However, there is a flow to the structure that I think will make sense in terms of building a complete picture of the current state of strength-based approaches to coaching leaders within organizations. Chapter 1 is all about context. There is an often-repeated myth that positive psychology began at the beginning of this century when in fact these ideas were being discussed 50 years earlier. So why didn't they gain traction? There are significant barriers to adopting a more positive mindset and these are discussed in this chapter. Chapter 2 is all about models. The concept of strengths is at an early stage of development so, unsurprisingly, there is some healthy debate about whether this construct is a state, trait, potential or something in-between. This debate matters, as how the strength construct is defined determines how it is assessed and developed. Chapter 3 introduces the theories behind the strength-based approach to leadership development. Positive leadership theories can be either explicit, eg authentic or transformational leadership, or implicit including growth mindsets and developmental readiness. Implicit theories matter as they shape our behaviour and attitudes towards the possibility of developing leadership behaviours in ourselves and others. Chapter 4 reviews some of the psychometric instruments that attempt to measure strengths and considers their reliability and their validity in terms of predicting performance. I also consider here the importance of the distinction between self-report versus multi-source feedback together with the validity of other forms of data including the peak experiences interview. Chapter 5 is all about the evidence for positive approaches to leadership development. This reviews not only the latest research (including my own) for the effectiveness of leadership coaching but also the evidence from other positive leadership studies.

The second half of the book is about applying the concepts and theories acquired in the first. Chapter 6 addresses one of the core challenges of strength-based leadership coaching. Once you have identified your strengths, how do you develop them? This partly depends on how developed the strength already is, whether it is over- or underutilized, or whether, if applied incorrectly and out of context, it has the potential to be a career derailer. Chapter 7 is about implementing a strength-based leadership coaching programme within an organization. Are the organization and the individuals within ready for change? Who are the key stakeholders? And what type of process will support the strength-based content? In addition the concept of measuring the outcomes of a coaching programme and determining the return on investment is addressed here. Chapter 8 is for leaders and managers who are interested in extending their strength-based capacities beyond leadership coaching. How do you both develop as a strength-based leader as coach and extend this mindset into recruitment, engagement, appraisals and beyond? Chapter 9 introduces the strength-based approach to team development. As most of us work in teams and depend on a high performing team to support our own performance, how do we integrate the strength-based approach to team structures, team leadership and a positive team process? Finally, Chapter 10 addresses the issues that many books on leadership and coaching choose to ignore: that is, what are the context and limitations of a strength-based approach? There has been a variety of criticisms aimed at positive and strength-based approaches and these must be appreciated and addressed if the strength-based approach is to develop and grow. Finally, I end with my thoughts on what best practice strength-based leadership coaching in organizations looks like from my perspective.

If you have any questions, comments or feedback, please get in touch at info@csaconsulting.biz.

ACKNOWLEDGEMENTS

This book is dedicated to Callum and Kaitlyn in the hope that the workforce they enter will be that bit more inspiring, encouraging and distributed in its leadership and consequently more conducive to a flourishing career.

The research upon which this book is predicated was supported by a number of talented leadership coaches including Ken Whitters, Linda McDonald, Lynn Scoles, Ernie Antoine, Mac Hay, Julie Edwards, Louise Klein, Joan Johnson, Patrea O'Donohue and Elise Sullivan, all of whom gave their time generously. The organizational sponsors, Lisa Greenfield and Tony McKimmie, were also very instrumental in maintaining participant engagement and supporting the research process.

Others who have provided encouragement and inspiration along the way include my collegues Warren Kennaugh, Dr Paul Flaxman, Ross Anderson, Katherine Tulpa, the Association for Coaching research group, and especially my mentor Prof David Clutterbuck. I would also like to thank the Association for Coaching for their unswerving support and belief that my research and writing made a significant contribution to the profession. Finally, sincere thanks to all the editorial staff at Kogan Page who backed the proposal, commented on the various drafts and helped shape it into the current publication.

An introduction to strength-based approaches in organizations

01

CHAPTER OVERVIEW

This chapter covers:

- The challenges of contemporary leadership development
- Historical overview of the strength-based approach
- What lies behind the focus on the negative?
- The evolution of leadership behaviour
- Approaches to talent and its management
- Current trends in positive leadership theory and development
- Coaching and positive psychology
- Definitions of positive leadership
- Rationale for a strength-based approach to developing leaders
- Basic tools of a strength-based approach
- Some questions to consider

The challenges of contemporary leadership development

Leadership and its development in organizations are in crisis. Despite the billions of dollars spent annually on the identification and development of leadership potential within organizations, the rate of manager and leader derailment remains at an estimated 50–70 per cent, the average CEO tenure is now 4.8 years, and high profile failures of corporate leadership continue to dominate the news nearly a decade after the global financial crisis exposed the fault lines in so many corporate structures. So what's going on? Why isn't the leadership development industry addressing these issues and identifying and developing leaders of the necessary calibre to lead effectively in 21st-century corporations?

Clearly there are multiple factors involved here. Leadership development consumes an estimated $50 billion annually (Bolden, 2007) in the United States alone and yet many programmes lack a substantial evidence base or comprehensive underpinning theory of leadership (Briner, 2012). Crucially it is still not apparent what specific elements of leadership development are effective so the majority of courses take a heterogeneous approach where multiple elements are combined in the hope that some are generally effective and a few are specifically instructive for individuals engaging in leadership development. This results in a general convergence of topics and processes on leadership programmes. Secondly there is the transfer problem. How do the leadership learnings on off-site Leadership Development Programmes (LDPs) get transferred back into the workplace? How are they integrated and appropriately utilized when the leader is back in their substantive role? This is a major issue as estimates of the amount of training that actually get meaningfully utilized after a training process are often around the 10 per cent mark (Burke and Hutchins, 2007) and the frequent lack of rigorous evaluation after training makes even these low estimates unreliable.

The lack of rigorous evaluation after many leadership programmes also promotes other challenges. Insufficient data regarding the relative efficacy of the multitude of possible leadership development options makes it near impossible to select those elements with the greatest impact. There are many reasons why leadership programmes are not evaluated effectively. For example, when we evaluate leadership development, who do we ask and at what stage in the programme do we ask them? Change takes time to work its way through the organization from leadership behaviour to follower response to team effectiveness and finally to organizational result. Consequently, most programmes only assess satisfaction with the leadership programme immediately after delivery and this is a very poor predictor of sustainable change in leadership behaviour. Without sufficient evaluation data it comes down to the preferences of the programme sponsor and the sales capacity of the programme provider to determine the content and structure of leadership programmes.

And yet leadership theories are developing, often in isolation from leadership development practices. Theories have come a long way from the great man approaches that emphasized the primacy of inherited traits to situational models that paid more attention to the context in which leadership behaviours were manifest to the positive models of authentic and transformational leadership we see today. The relative isolation of leadership theory development (often in academic settings) positively promotes the proliferation of fads and trends in the leadership development domain that have little or no empirical substantiation. This research–practitioner divide blocks the development of effective leadership development processes as academic theories are denied empirical testing in organizations, and practitioner models often develop with minimal empirical substantiation. Look at mindfulness, for example. There are now many leadership programmes that incorporate this into their modules but, despite the intuitive links between attentiveness and leadership performance, none of these associations have yet been demonstrated empirically. Positive models of leadership development offer the opportunity to bring some rigour and innovation into the leadership development process.

A history of positive approaches

Despite a brief hiatus in the early 20th century, the focus of development in organizations has been overwhelmingly on the negative (Wright and Quick, 2009). The hiatus was led in part by humanistic psychologists like Maslow (1954) whose hierarchy of needs remains with us today. Less well remembered was his focus on the positive (he even coined the term 'positive psychology'), peak experiences and human potential. His list of qualities of self-actualized people looks very similar to some contemporary models of virtues and character strengths (Peterson and Seligman, 2004). Despite this flourishing of ideas, Maslow and other humanistic psychologists were criticized for their lack of empirical rigour and the lack of the development of an evidence base to support their theories seems to explain in part why this approach failed to gain traction in organizations.

Positive approaches in applied psychology including leadership resurfaced when Martin Seligman dedicated his presidency of the American Psychological Association to happiness, excellence and optimal human functioning (Seligman and Csikszentmihalyi, 2000). Positive psychology focused on the three pillars of inquiry: positive subjective experiences, traits like character strengths and positive institutions. Each of these areas began to develop their own research base but the penetration of these ideas into the workplace was limited at least in part because of the lack of developability of trait-like constructs and the lack of explicit links from subjective experiences to enhanced organizational performance.

Slowly the domain of positive organization psychology (POP) began to evolve but progress was limited for a variety of reasons. Firstly, the three pillars of positive psychology did not align perfectly with the organizational need for developable strengths and talents with explicit links to enhanced organizational effectiveness (Money, Hillenbrand and da Camara, 2008). Secondly, evidence emerged that individuals in organizations were unaware of their strengths (Kaplan and Kaiser, 2010) so some of the foundational elements for a science of POP were not yet visible in organizations. Thirdly, early research in POP was primarily cross-sectional, partial and heavily reliant on self-report data (Mills, Fleck and Kozikowski, 2013). This meant that research could only suggest correlations with positive constructs and desired organizational metrics and that individual ratings of well-being and performance were privileged over what peers, colleagues and bosses actually saw in terms of changes in leadership behaviour and productivity. Finally, as is the case in many evolving paradigms, there was some conceptual confusion as to the structure of positive models in organizations. Early models of positive functioning in organizations included the CHOSE model (standing for confidence, hope, optimism, subjective well-being and emotional intelligence (Luthans, 2002)). However, not all of those components gained traction in organizations or instead, like emotional intelligence, developed their own research domain (see box below).

Is emotional intelligence part of POP?

Emotional intelligence is defined as the identification and management of emotions in self and others. There are many models of emotional intelligence, including ability and competency based, and emotional awareness has been suggested as a strength (Linley, Harrington and Garcea, 2010). However, there are challenges in measuring this construct with the obvious paradox that it requires emotional intelligence to rate yourself accurately on emotional intelligence inventories. Consequently self-report inventories risk significant overratings from those who are unskilled or unaware. Despite being initially suggested as a core element of positive organizational behaviour, there has been little cross-fertilization between the two domains, with both POP and EI following separate if parallel research trajectories. Whilst EI does share some similarities with POP, the focus is not necessarily on the positive and there is the risk that emotional awareness in leaders can be used for coercive rather than altruistic motives. For these reasons, EI is not currently considered part of the POP agenda.

Nonetheless, positive leadership development offers access to a range of new theoretical and evidence-based approaches that have the potential to refine and enhance how leaders and leadership are developed. There are several contemporary research foci in positive organizational psychology that can inform positive leadership development. These can be divided into two major strands of research that feed into the positive organizational psychology paradigm. Positive organizational behaviour (POB) was articulated as a research-based, measurable and state-like approach that consequently could be targeted for development in organizations (Luthans and Youssef, 2007). A contrasting approach to this has been defined as positive organizational scholarship (POS) which examines positive deviant behaviour from a more trait-like perspective. The POS focus on the classification and identification of virtues like compassion and gratitude (Boyatzis, Smith and Blaize, 2006) in organizations lends itself more to selection than development processes. This state–trait debate runs through the field of POP and is clearly apparent in the differing approaches to the utilization of strengths with the POS approach favouring the 'identify and use' approach where awareness and leverage are sufficient to enhance performance, and the POB orientation supporting the notion of 'strengths development' where a more sophisticated and nuanced approach is taken to performance enhancement (Biswas-Diener, Kashdan and Minhas, 2011). This link between the type of positive construct assessed and how it is subsequently developed is a crucial aspect of strength-based leadership development.

The POB approach has also been developed in conjunction with the concept of Psychological Capital (PsyCap) where positive emotions like confidence, hope, optimism and resiliency are seen as essential prerequisites to developing a positive leadership style (Avolio and Luthans, 2006). By contrast, POS has maintained its focus at the more macro-organizational level through the investigation of positively deviant organizations and virtuousness or eudaemonism (Cameron, 2008). POS is consequently more interested in the identification of virtues that are seen as inherently good rather than necessarily linked to improved performance and includes well-being rather than just job performance as a desired organizational outcome (Fineman, 2006). Figure 1.1 illustrates how positive psychology links to these positive organizational concepts.

The separation of POP into these two separate and conceptually distinct research domains into those that chose to focus on positive organizational behaviour (POB) and those that preferred to focus on positive institutions (Positive Organizational Scholarship, or POS) has caused some challenges in the development of positive models in organizations. The distinction may seem somewhat arbitrary and potentially reflective more of the interests of the researchers concerned than any natural fault lines in POP. Nonetheless, it matters as the assumptions, level of analysis and models behind each approach

FIGURE 1.1 The links between positive psychology and organizational psychology (from MacKie, 2015)

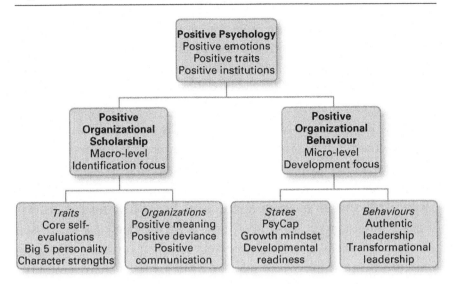

are significantly different and have led to different research programmes that have contrasting inherent models for organizational, including leadership, development. Figure 1.1 illustrates the development of the various strands of positive organizational behaviour.

However, gradually these issues are being addressed in POP, and several strands of research have emerged and are developing significant empirical support. These include the investigation of Psychological Capital, or PsyCap for short (hope, optimism, self-efficacy and resilience), and its links with emotional contagion, follower positivity and performance (Meyers, van Woerkom and Bakker, 2013; Meyers *et al*, 2015). In addition, strength identification and development has generated a lot of interest, with whole novel taxonomies of strengths and virtues being developed as well as methodologies for developing them (Biswas-Diener, Kashdan and Minhas, 2011). Of all the developing areas, however, it is positive leadership that is generating the most interest and greatest research impact (Donaldson and Ko, 2010). These models include authentic, transformational, altruistic and servant leadership.

The positive psychology framework is not without its critics and these need to be considered when applying its constructs to the development of leadership. Only the most proselytizing ideological proponents advocate a complete focus on the positive with no attention to deficits or derailers. However, the ideal ratio of positive to negative emotions has been vigorously debated with the Losada and Heaphy (2004) ratio in high performing teams at 5:1 ratio of positive to negative communication recently challenged (Brown, Sokal and Friedman, 2013). Other researchers have argued for the importance of negative emotions and stressed their evolutionary origins as adaptations to loss and threat (Gilbert, 2006). In addition, there is also an ongoing concern that strengths can be overdone and that all strengths, if leveraged without regard to context or impact, will become derailers (Kaiser, 2009). Given that many people already overestimate their competence on a wide variety of tasks (Dunning *et al*, 2003) there is also the risk that an unrelenting focus on the positive further distorts intrapersonal perceptions and reaffirms preexisting positive biases. As self-awareness requires increasing recognition and alignment between the perceptions of self and others, the exclusive emphasis on the personal and the positive would appear to be antithetical to the development of self-insight, one of the cornerstones of multiple models of leadership development (Avolio, 2010). Finally, there is the risk that a focus on strengths becomes just another trait-based approach to developing individuals and organizations and ignores the complex interplay of personal qualities with team, group and dyadic and situational variables (Hernandez *et al*, 2011). These criticisms in their totality clearly argue for a balanced and considered approach to the application of positive psychology constructs to the leadership development domain where the limitations of a blinkered and partial approach to positivity are clearly recognized and avoided. These risks and limits of a strength-based approach are more fully explored in Chapter 10.

What lies behind the focus on the negative?

Why, despite early evidence that happy workers were more productive (Wright and Quick, 2009), did this negative mindset in organizational and leadership development prevail until the beginning of this century? One answer is that negative emotions are adaptive.

They narrow our behavioural repertoires and promote fast track thinking that can literally save our lives (Gilbert, 2006). By contrast, the evolutionary adaptiveness of positive emotions, apart from their inherent sense of subjective well-being, is less apparent. So the evidence base behind the functionality of positive emotions in the workplace was slower to accumulate and therefore less compelling as a rationale for change. In addition, there is evidence that our own biases promote the focus on the negative and these derive from our evolutionary history (Nesse, 2005). The 'smoke detector principle' explains why we both experience significant amounts of negative emotion, even in the absence of overt threats, and pay a disproportionate amount of attention to them. So, thinking functionally about negative emotions, it's worthwhile enduring all the false alarms just to accurately anticipate the one time there may be a threat. This negativity bias is confirmed by other research that demonstrates that it is much easier to learn to be fearful and acquire aversions than it is to develop a positive association (Rozin and Royzman, 2001). Indeed these fears and phobias can often be acquired in just a single negative event. Combine this with our capacity to maintain these fears through our own distorted thinking and reflect on the number of descriptors we have for negative emotions versus positive ones, and you can see why strength-based approaches have struggled to gain traction. Transferring this thinking to the workplace, it may appear worthwhile focusing on the leadership deficits as a matter of course, just in case that missing capability proves a fatal career derailer. Of course, this approach is both inefficient, in that it targets environmental threats and challenges that may never emerge, and wasteful, in that developmental time and energy goes into plugging gaps rather than developing strengths.

However, the strength of this deficit focus is partially mediated by the profession within which the individual leader resides. Law, for example, is well known for its high rates of depression and dissatisfaction. And yet legal pessimism in proportion can be adaptive. I once worked with a legal partner who told me that missing one word in a contract had cost the firm $1 million. Clearly there are times when hyper-vigilance and attention to detail can be organizationally adaptive if somewhat personally challenging.

The evolution of leadership behaviour

There are several ways in which evolutionary theory can inform our understanding of leadership.

Firstly, we need to understand the origins or phylogeny of leadership behaviour. The evolutionary model states leadership behaviour evolved to solve an adaptive problem, namely how does a group reach consensus about shared activities? Many species addressed this problem by evolving dominance hierarchies, but this was unlikely to be the case in early humans as there is little correlation between dominance and leadership and, in fact, the anthropological evidence suggests humans were fiercely egalitarian in their hunter-gatherer phase (Boehm, 1999). Importantly human leadership behaviour evolved as the complexity of the social environment increased. According to van Vugt, Hogan and Kaiser (2008), there are four distinct stages of development in the evolution of human leadership behaviour, ranging from prehuman, where dominance hierarchies were the norm, to egalitarian hunter-gatherer bands, where leadership crucially shifted from intimidation to attraction demonstrating situational and prestige-based leadership structures. Only with the invention of agriculture about 13,000 years ago did populations grow and settle, promoting the development of formalized, central and hierarchical models of leadership that only gave way to corporate leadership around 250 years ago with the gradual development of more fluid, participatory and inclusive models of leadership. This evolutionary perspective is important if you consider that for 99 per cent of the history of our species we have been living in an egalitarian hunter-gatherer environment and many of our cognitive adaptations like the theory of mind (ie knowing that followers also have intentions and drives), language and culture evolved in this domain. Consequently the often repeated and status quo justifying the assertion that humans have always lived in hierarchies is simply not supported by the evidence.

So evolutionary models inform us that corporate leadership is, historically speaking, a very recent development, with the majority of human prehistory being spent in small, egalitarian communities with active reverse-dominance hierarchies. It also confirms that leadership does not equal dominance; humans have been primarily egalitarian in their history and there is no biological justification for organizational hierarchies. This type of assertion not only commits the naturalistic fallacy (that is, attempting to describe naturally occurring phenomena as the way things should and must be) but also is not supported by the anthropological evidence. Organizational hierarchies are a cultural phenomenon and vary significantly across countries and organizations. They are not hard-wired into our DNA and are capable of radical transformations.

Secondly, leadership theories have significantly evolved and developed over time. There has been a general trend from the simple to the complex and also a move away from unitary models that focus on only one factor like extraversion to models that express multiple capabilities like transformational leadership. The evolution of these models changes the focus of leadership development from skill development to empowerment, collaboration and a focus on teams. In addition, there is a trend away from leaders and towards leadership that is more distributed and shared (Crevani, Lindgren and Packendorff, 2010). Strength-based models are entirely consistent with this distributed approach that suggests much untapped potential lies within each individual.

Finally, leadership evolves during the lifetime of the individual (ontogeny) with leaders potentially moving through several stages of maturation and cognitive development (Kegan, 1994). Each level can offer a greater perspective and shifts thinking from the categorical to the reflective and systemic modalities (Berger and Atkins, 2009). These models also find support in the concept of levelized competencies which make the case for the development of specific capabilities as leaders progress up an organizational hierarchy. We'll have more to say about how strength-based approaches align with these concepts of individual maturity and development in Chapter 10.

The epigenetics of talent

Partially because of a misunderstanding about the evolutionary origins of leadership that mistakenly equated evolved with innate, talent management, like much of applied psychology, has for decades laboured under the perennial dichotomies of state versus trait, genetic versus environment and born versus made. These dichotomies have left a powerful legacy in the way we think about fundamental concepts like talent or strengths today. However, recent research has thankfully challenged this either/or mindset and instead suggested a more integrative and complex approach (Clutterbuck, 2012).

In addition, the pendulum swing towards the positive perspective was also happening in the field of talent management. A number of attempts have been made to more fully articulate the assumptions that underpin contemporary talent management practices (Meyers and van Woerkom, 2014). These assumptions appear to converge around themes of talent scarcity versus ubiquity, malleability versus rigidity and innate versus acquired. The strength-based approach received support from a greater focus on leadership as a more distributed, trainable and acquired capability that alerted organizations to the untapped potential within their emerging leaders (Meyers, van Woerkom and Dries, 2013).

The epigenetics of talent is an important extension of the traditional binary genes versus environment description. Epigenetics is the study of what switches genes on and off to modify their expression. Environmental factors that can switch genes on and off include diet, drugs, ageing and possibly stress (Spector, 2012). So genes are not destiny: talented individuals can be curtailed by an unsupportive or impoverished environment and talent can be amplified by epigenetic manipulation. This discovery undermines one of the three pillars of the traditional talent management stool, that talent is innate, scarce and should be competed for rather than developed (Meyers *et al*, 2013). Concurrent with these biological revelations were and are the notion that leadership is no longer the preserve of the privileged few but much more effective if shared, distributed and cascaded throughout an organization (Hawkins, 2011). To date we have little concept of what switches leadership capacity on and off within individuals, but we do know that leaders that display extraordinary capability in one organization can struggle when they transfer to another (Groysberg, 2012).

Origins of a more positive approach to leadership

Leadership and its development is a subset of talent management and benefitted from the realization that talent was much more present and malleable than originally thought. In addition, the positive psychology movement also sponsored this transformational shift in perspective. Although it was Martin Seligman's address to the American Psychological Society (Seligman, 2000) at the start of the new millennium that turned applied psychology on its axis and reorientated it towards what was flourishing, successful and effective in human endeavours, the origins of a more positive approach to leadership and organizations was much older. Humanistic psychologists such as Maslow and Rogers (eg Maslow, 1954) had advocated the ideological and theoretical focus on human strengths and potential but struggled to provide the necessary empirical and experimental support that other paradigms like behaviourism were capable of producing (Boakes, 1984).

So what stops the positive and strength-based approaches to leadership development being just another fad in the leadership development business? Firstly, positive approaches are theoretically supported both by existing models like transformational leadership (one of the most researched and validated models there is (Judge and Piccolo, 2004)) as well as new and emerging models of positive leadership like authentic leadership. Secondly, positive leadership is integrated with the existing leadership development literature. It seeks to extend existing well validated and reliable models rather than propose an entirely new and exclusive approach. Thirdly, positive research is being empirically verified through carefully controlled experiments that are teasing out the active components of positive leadership interventions (MacKie, 2014).

Positive leadership models drew on two distinct strands of positive organizational psychology. Firstly, positive organizational behaviour (POB) evolved with its focus on measureable state-like constructs like optimism, that could be targeted for developmental purposes (Luthans and Youssef, 2007). POB has been defined as 'the study and application of positively orientated human resource strengths and psychological capacities that can be measured, developed and effect-ively managed for performance improvement in today's workplace' (Luthans, 2002) and is well aligned with positive leadership develop-ment. The contrasting positive organizational scholarship focused on the classification and identification of more trait-like constructs like virtues. This approach lent itself more to selection than development. Positive leadership is largely an extension of the POB approach due to its focus on skills and states that can be developed and are malle-able to targeted interventions. The POB approach has led to a number of research areas including psychological capital (Luthans *et al*, 2007), authentic leadership (Day *et al*, 2014) and leadership coaching (MacKie, 2014). The POS approach has focused mainly on character strengths and virtues (Peterson and Seligman, 2004) and positively deviant organizations (Cameron, 2008). These distinctions are not arbitrary and arcane academic classifications but have real impact in the world of leadership development in organizations. If you believe that leadership is trait-based then you do all you can to positively select those traits. Your talent management strategy then becomes one of competing for those who manifest those traits. If you believe that leadership is composed of more state-like constructs then you focus more on the development of those states and less on competing at the level of selection. So implicit models, beliefs and mindsets around leadership really matter as they shape behaviour in the lead-ership development process.

Contemporary trends in positive leadership theory

There is now a recognition amongst many leadership experts (Day, Harrison and Halpin, 2012) that leadership (and not leaders) is the necessary focus for contemporary theorizing and leadership applica-tion. This swing from the individual to the collective has been medi-ated in part by the recognition that the sheer scale and complexity of many extant leadership roles in organizations make them beyond the capacity of any single individual and instead requiring the collective capability of a high performing team (Hawkins, 2011). Secondly, positive leadership theories are increasingly integrating moral and ethical concerns into their sub-domains, eg authentic leadership. This is no accident that these models have emerged after the global financial crisis where the absence of ethical concerns are thought to have significantly contributed to reckless and self-serving decision-making. Positive leadership theories are more fully discussed in Chapter 3.

Contemporary trends in positive leadership development

Leadership development is also evolving and three trends in particular are relevant for our focus on strength-based approaches. Firstly, leadership development has become individualized, tailored to the needs of the individual and designed as a bespoke intervention delivered through an executive or leadership coaching process. This is a significant shift from the training approaches that dominated leadership development where the leader was required to fit the curriculum rather than the other way around. It's not immediately apparent what triggered this shift, but part of the pull factor was the fact that leadership programmes varied enormously in their efficacy (Avolio *et al*, 2009) and individual leader factors, like developmental readiness and openness to experience, were found to moderate the success of such programmes (Avolio and Hannah, 2008). It made sense therefore to tailor programmes to work with the individual capabilities of the leader rather than shoehorning them into a one-size-fits-all programme.

Secondly, leadership development began adopting a more positive orientation, away from the traditional deficit approach that identified gaps on a leadership survey and built a development plan around addressing those gaps to moderate the success of such programmes (Meyers *et al*, 2015). In many cases, this positive approach complemented rather than supplanted the deficit orientation and built on existing models of engagement like the Job Characteristics Model that emphasized autonomy, significance and feedback (Mills, Fleck and Kozikowski, 2013).

Thirdly, leadership development began incorporating the concept of levelized competencies where more senior leaders were required to have significantly different capabilities from their more junior counterparts (Lord and Hall, 2005; Mumford *et al*, 2005). This differentiation by level has been described in a number of different formats. Lord and Hall (2005) integrated leadership development into a model of developing expertise, suggesting that novice level leaders focused largely on technical mastery whereas more senior leaders tended to focus on authentic and value-based leadership. Mumford *et al* (2005) took a different approach creating a leadership strataplex that consisted of cognitive, interpersonal, business and strategic domains. Cognitive skills, like processing information, are seen as being most in evidence at more junior levels within an organization. The business and strategic requirements, like planning, financial management and visioning are, by contrast, in much greater demand at more senior leadership levels.

Finally, leadership development became more practical, applied and experiential with suggestions that effective leadership development should follow the 70:20:10 model, with 70 per cent of leadership development coming from on-the-job experiences, 20 per cent coming from mentoring and coaching, and only 10 per cent from formal training programmes (Lombardo and Eichinger, 2007).

A more individualized, levelized, experiential and positive approach to leadership development fundamentally challenged traditional pedagogic models of leadership training. Individualized coaching was ready and able to fill the niche created by these developments, led in many cases by psychologists with expertise in individualized psychological assessment and armed with change management and behaviour modification skills honed in the face of complex and intransigent clinical disorders.

Coaching and positive psychology

Coaching and positive psychology have emerged and developed at similar times to the point where multiple authors have suggested they are intimately connected and mutually compatible (Grant and Cavanagh, 2007; Linley, Woolston and Biswas-Diener, 2009). Coaching has been seen as both an applied manifestation of positive psychology and a mechanism to translate theoretical positive constructs into action (Freire, 2013). Both coaching and positive psychology share certain assumptions in their focus on the positive, the belief that people want to learn and most importantly that individuals contain within themselves, the solution to their own challenges. This apparent consanguinity has led to models of coaching, like authentic happiness coaching, that explicitly focus on the development of the three pillars of positive psychology, namely pleasure, engagement and meaning (Kauffman, 2006). However, differences are beginning to emerge in part due to environmental events, like the global financial crisis which prompted coaching to reexamine some of its foundational assumptions. After all, many of the failed institutions of that era were heavy users of executive coaching so why, in that case, were so many poor decisions made and leadership so clearly compromised (Blakey and Day, 2012)? Although initially coaching models were content neutral and merely provided a framework for the coachees' own self-exploration, there are now emerging specialist models of coaching, including leadership coaching, that require expertise on behalf of the coach and can be much more directive in their approach (Elliott, 2011). Coaching has subsequently become one of the key delivery mechanisms of positive leadership development (Day *et al*, 2014).

What's the definition of positive leadership?

To be included in the positive leadership approach, leadership theories require four elements:

1 Firstly, a focus on the leaders' personal and situational strengths is required to understand their peak performance and the qualities that support this. This is combined with a growth mindset that change and development is possible.

2 Secondly, the leadership model needs to have a positive impact on those around the leader, especially the followers. Leadership is a relational process and the benefits of positive leadership cannot be confined to the individual.

3 Thirdly, the positive impact on others needs to translate into meaningful increases in organizational objectives like extra discretionary effort and enhanced organizational performance. They may be happier followers but they must also be more productive.

4 Finally, the purpose of positive leadership is self-transcendent and not coercive in the manipulation of others for personal gain. Positive leadership models contain within them a clear focus on ethical decision-making and behaviour that transcend self-serving gratifications in the leader.

Rationale for a strength-based approach to leadership development

So leadership has evolved for surviving not thriving and we are pre-disposed to seek and focus on the negative in many aspects of our organizational lives. The challenge with this evolutionary history is that it makes knowing our strengths, focusing on the positives and unlocking the potential that is overlooked with the traditional deficit approach that much harder. However the opportunities provided by a strength-based approach to leadership development are significant. The rationale for this approach is clear and compelling. Firstly, the focus on strengths seeks to redress the traditional deficit reduction focus on leadership development (Luthans and Avolio, 2003). Secondly, meta-analytic outcome studies show that current leadership models are unable to explain significant amounts of variance suggesting there are many more critical variables to be discovered in the field of leadership development (Avolio *et al*, 2009). Thirdly, practitioner application of the strength-based approach appears to be significantly ahead of the research evidence making it an opportune time to review the status of the current evidentiary base (Donaldson and Ko, 2010). Finally, positive psychology constructs have been successfully applied in other domains, including clinical psychology, suggesting the assessment of their cross-domain application is warranted and timely (Seligman *et al*, 2005).

It can be seen that positive leadership development including strength-based approaches is part of a broader trend that advocates a more inclusive and developmental approach to leadership talent. These distributed models raise engagement and unlock talent as they challenge the assumption that leadership is the privilege of the select few and advocate a broader distribution of capability within an organization. The strength-based approach to leadership is therefore more egalitarian and participative, helping to develop and retain employees. These distributed models align well with the move away from the unsustainable focus on heroic leader qualities. In addition to developing leaders and leadership, strength-based approaches also help develop engagement and psychological capital in their followers which in turn enhances performance (van Woerkom and Meyers, 2014). Strength-based approaches have the capacity to enhance the working lives and effectiveness of all employees by helping them raise awareness of their strengths, align them with the needs of the organization and build mastery in leadership capability. Used skilfully and wisely, strength-based approaches have the capacity to transform leadership capability within organizations.

Tools to help understand strength-based approaches

It is worth introducing some fundamental concepts in the lexicon of strength-based approaches at an early stage in our exploration of the concept. The notion of mindsets is foundational to understanding and applying positive leadership development. Mindsets are fundamental ways we appraise the world and our capacity to shape and influence it. One of the most commonly cited mindsets is the growth versus fixed approach to learning and development. This is because it challenges the fixed or entity model of leadership and other capabilities like intelligence and instead views them as potentials to be developed. This shifts the focus from strengths independent of context to strengths that are embedded in contexts and don't meaningfully exist in isolation. It also forces us to consider how leadership strengths are developed and the readiness and belief in positive capability change that predicate and moderate successful leadership development. Some authors have even argued that utilization is key with under- or overutilization no longer definable as strengths (Niemiec, 2014).

A second key concept is the notion that strengths exist in a variety of formats from traits, talents, capabilities and states with each category requiring specific developmental processes and approaches. States like confidence and self-efficacy are relatively easy to develop, aligned with positive leadership principles and have a demonstrable impact on performance. Traits like integrity and conscientiousness are much harder to develop and, as a consequence, are rarely the focus of leadership coaching interventions. This distinction will be further explored in the assessment of strengths reviewed in Chapter 4.

Conclusion

Positive leadership development, including strength-based approaches, offers at least a partial antidote to addressing some of the contemporary challenges of effective leadership development. Firstly, it offers access to a range of new theoretical and evidence-based approaches that have the potential to significantly enhance the effectiveness of leadership development in organizations. Secondly, it offers a welcome counterbalance to the traditional deficit focus in leadership development (Luthans and Avolio, 2003) that is itself predicated on our evolutionary preparedness to orientate towards threat and negativity. Thirdly, it offers an opportunity to close the research–practitioner gap making practitioners more accountable and leadership programmes more effective and evidence-based.

Some questions to consider

- What factors have maintained the deficit focus in organizations?
- What does our environment of evolutionary adaptation tell us about our propensities and preadaptations for leadership?

- Is there such an entity as a natural leader? What are the consequences of such implicit models and categorizations?

- How does the assessment of strengths affect their development? Does it matter if the strength you try and develop is trait-like or state-like?

References

Avolio, B J (ed) (2010) *Full Range Leadership Development*, SAGE Publications, Thousand Oaks, CA

Avolio, B J and Luthans, F (2006) *The High Impact Leader*, McGraw-Hill, New York

Avolio, B J and Hannah, S T (2008) Developmental readiness: accelerating leader development, *Consulting Psychology Journal: Practice and Research*, 60 (4), pp 331–47

Avolio, B J *et al* (2009) A meta-analytic review of leadership impact research: experimental and quasi-experimental studies, *The Leadership Quarterly*, 20 (5), pp 764–84

Berger, J G and Atkins, P W B (2009) Mapping complexity of mind: using the subject-object interview in coaching, *Coaching: An International Journal of Theory, Research and Practice*, 2 (1), pp 23–36

Biswas-Diener, R, Kashdan, T B and Minhas, G (2011) A dynamic approach to psychological strength development and intervention, *Journal of Positive Psychology*, 6 (2), pp 106–18

Blakey, J and Day, I (2012) *Challenging Coaching: Going beyond traditional coaching to face the FACTS*, Nicholas Brealey Publishing, London

Boakes, R (1984) *From Darwin to Behaviourism: Psychology and the minds of animals*, Cambridge University Press Archive

Boehm, C (1999) *Hierarchy in the Forest: The evolution of egalitarian behavior*, Harvard University Press, Cambridge, MA

Bolden, R (2007) Trends and perspectives in management and leadership development, *Business Leadership Review*, 4 (2), pp 1–13

Boyatzis, R E, Smith, M L and Blaize, N (2006) Developing sustainable leaders through coaching and compassion, *Academy of Management Learning and Education*, 5 (1), pp 8–24

Briner, R B (2012) Does coaching work and does anyone really care? *OP Matters 16*, pp 4–11

Brown, N J L, Sokal, A D and Friedman, H L (2013) The complex dynamics of wishful thinking: the critical positivity ratio, *American Psychologist*, 68 (9), pp 801–13

Burke, L A and Hutchins, H M (2007) Training transfer: an integrative literature review, *Human Resource Development Review*, **6** (3), pp 263–96

Cameron, K S (2008) *Positive Leadership: Strategies for extraordinary performance*, Berrett-Koehler Publishers, San Francisco, CA

Clutterbuck, D (2012) *The Talent Wave: Why succession planning fails and what to do about it*, Kogan Page, London

Crevani, L, Lindgren, M and Packendorff, J (2010) Leadership, not leaders: on the study of leadership as practices and interactions, *Scandinavian Journal of Management*, **26**, pp 77–86

Day, D V, Harrison, M M and Halpin, S M (2012) *An Integrative Approach to Leader Development: Connecting adult development, identity, and expertise*, Routledge, New York

Day, D V *et al* (2014) Advances in leader and leadership development: a review of 25 years of research and theory, *The Leadership Quarterly*, **25** (1), pp 63–82

Donaldson, S I and Ko, I (2010) Positive organizational psychology, behavior, and scholarship: a review of the emerging literature and evidence base, *The Journal of Positive Psychology*, **5** (3), pp 177–91

Dunning, D *et al* (2003) Why people fail to recognize their own incompetence, *Current Directions in Psychological Science*, **12** (3), pp 83–87

Elliott, R (2011) Utilising evidence-based leadership theories in coaching for leadership development: towards a comprehensive integrating conceptual framework, *International Coaching Psychology Review*, **6** (1), pp 46–70

Fineman, S (2006) On being positive: concerns and counterpoints, *Academy of Management Review*, **31** (2), pp 270–91

Freire, T (2013) Positive psychology approaches, *The Wiley–Blackwell Handbook of the Psychology of Coaching and Mentoring*, pp 426–42

Gilbert, P (2006) Evolution and depression: issues and implications, *Psychological Medicine*, **36** (3), pp 287–97

Grant, A M and Cavanagh, M J (2007) Evidence-based coaching: flourishing or languishing?, *Australian Psychologist*, **42** (4), pp 239–54

Groysberg, B (2012) *Chasing Stars: The myth of talent and the portability of performance*, Princeton University Press, Princeton, NJ

Hawkins, P (2011) *Leadership Team Coaching: Developing collective transformational leadership*, Kogan Page, London

Hernandez, M *et al* (2011) The loci and mechanisms of leadership: exploring a more comprehensive view of leadership theory, *The Leadership Quarterly*, **22** (6), pp 1165–85

Judge, T A and Piccolo, R F (2004) Transformational and transactional leadership: a meta-analytic test of their relative validity, *Journal of Applied Psychology*, **89** (5), pp 755–68

Kaiser, R B (ed) (2009) *The Perils of Accentuating the Positive*, Hogan Press, Tulsa, OK

Kaplan, R E and Kaiser, R B (2010) Toward a positive psychology for leaders, in *Oxford Handbook of Positive Psychology and Work*, eds P A Linley, S Harrington and N Garcea, Oxford University Press, New York

Kauffman, C (2006) Positive psychology: the science at the heart of coaching, *Evidence Based Coaching Handbook: Putting best practices to work for your clients*, eds D R Stober and A M Grant, pp 219–53, Wiley, Hoboken, NJ

Kegan, R (1994) *In Over Our Heads: The mental demands of modern life*, Harvard University Press, Cambridge, MA

Linley, P A, Woolston, L and Biswas-Diener, R (2009) Strengths coaching with leaders, *International Coaching Psychology Review*, 4 (1), pp 37–48

Lombardo, M M and Eichinger, R W (2007) *The Leadership Machine: Architecture to develop leaders for any future*, Lominger International, Minneapolis, MN

Lord, R G and Hall, R J (2005) Identity, deep structure and the development of leadership skill, *The Leadership Quarterly*, 16 (4), pp 591–615

Losada, M and Heaphy, E (2004) The role of positivity and connectivity in the performance of business teams: a nonlinear dynamics model, *American Behavioral Scientist*, 47 (6), pp 740–65

Luthans, F (2002) The need for and meaning of positive organizational behavior, *Journal of Organizational Behavior*, 23 (6), pp 695–706

Luthans, F and Avolio, B J (2003) Authentic leadership: a positive developmental approach, in *Positive Organizational Scholarship*, eds K S Cameron, J E Dutton and R E Quinn, pp 241–61, Berrett-Koehler, Oakland, CA

Luthans, F and Youssef, C M (2007) Emerging positive organizational behavior, *Journal of Management*, 33 (3), pp 321–49

Luthans, F *et al* (2007) Positive psychological capital: measurement and relationship with performance and satisfaction, *Personnel Psychology*, 60 (3), pp 541–72

MacKie, D (2014) The effectiveness of strength-based executive coaching in enhancing full range leadership development: a controlled study, *Consulting Psychology Journal: Practice and Research*, 66 (2), pp 118–37

MacKie, D J (2015) Coaching for strength-based leadership, in *Leadership Coaching: Working with leaders to develop elite performance*, 2nd edn, ed J Passmore, pp 317–32, Kogan Page, London

Maslow, A H (1954) *Motivation and Personality*, Harper, New York

Meyers, M C, van Woerkom, M and Bakker, A B (2013) The added value of the positive: a literature review of positive psychology interventions in organizations, *European Journal of Work and Organizational Psychology*, 22 (5), pp 618–32

Meyers, M C, van Woerkom, M and Dries, N (2013) Talent – Innate or acquired? Theoretical considerations and their implications for talent management, *Human Resource Management Review*, 23 (4), pp 305–21

Meyers, M C and van Woerkom, M (2014) The influence of underlying philosophies on talent management: theory, implications for practice, and research agenda, *Journal of World Business*, 49 (2), pp 192–203

Meyers, M C *et al* (2015). Enhancing psychological capital and personal growth initiative: working on strengths or deficiencies, *Journal of Counseling Psychology*, 62 (1), pp 50–62

Mills, M J, Fleck, C R and Kozikowski, A (2013). Positive psychology at work: a conceptual review, state-of-practice assessment, and a look ahead, *The Journal of Positive Psychology*, 8 (2), pp 153–64

Money, K, Hillenbrand, C and da Camara, N (2008) Putting positive psychology to work in organisations, *Journal of General Management*, 34 (3), pp 21–36

Mumford, M D *et al* (2000) Development of leadership skills: experience and timing, *The Leadership Quarterly*, 11 (1), pp 87–114

Nesse, R (2005) Evolutionary psychology and mental health, in *The Handbook of Evolutionary Psychology*, ed D Buss, Wiley, Hoboken, NJ

Niemiec, R M (2014) *Mindfulness and Character Strengths: A practical guide to flourishing*, Hogrefe Verlag, Göttingen

Peterson, C and Seligman, M E P (2004) *Character Strengths and Virtues: A handbook and classification*, Oxford University Press, New York

Rozin, P and Royzman, E B (2001) Negativity bias, negativity dominance, and contagion, *Personality and Social Psychology Review*, 5 (4), pp 296–320

Seligman, M E P and Csikszentmihalyi, M (2000) Positive psychology: an introduction, *American Psychologist*, 55 (1), pp 5–14

Seligman, M E P *et al* (2005) Positive psychology progress: empirical validation of interventions, *American Psychologist*, 60 (5), pp 410–21

Spector, T (2012) *Identically Different: Why you can change your genes*, Hachette, London

van Vugt, M, Hogan, R and Kaiser, R B (2008) Leadership, followership, and evolution: some lessons from the past, *American Psychologist*, 63 (3), pp 182–96

van Woerkom, M and Meyers, M C (2014) My strengths count!, *Human Resource Management*, 54 (1), pp 81–103

Wright, T A and Quick, J C (2009) The emerging positive agenda in organizations: greater than a trickle, but not yet a deluge, *Journal of Organizational Behavior*, 30 (2), pp 147–59

Strengths
Definitions and models

02

CHAPTER OVERVIEW

This chapter covers:

- What is a strength? How theory shapes practice
- Existing strength models – domains, capacities, traits and process
- Looking at strengths across the state–trait continuum
- How do strengths link to performance?
- Strengths overdone
- Strengths in context
- Strengths and decision latitude

Introduction

Strengths are surprisingly hard to define, despite being near ubiquitous in the language of executive and leadership development. In considering strengths and how they impact on the development of leaders, there are some key questions to consider. Firstly, does the construct of 'strengths' have construct validity? That is, can it be defined in a meaningful way that has some explanatory power and predictive utility in the field of leadership development? Secondly, does the concept of strengths have discriminant validity? That is, does it measure something discretely different from other concepts like talents or preferences? Strengths have been defined as traits, capacities and predispositions, all of which then influence and determine how they are assessed and developed. Thirdly, does the concept of strengths have predictive validity? That is, does it tell us something useful about the potential and performance of the individual, team or organization? Finally, how does the concept of strengths link to performance, especially in a leadership context?

Definitions of strengths

- 'a trait that ideally is practised at an extremely high level, typical of the top 10 or 20 per cent of leaders in a given population' (Zenger *et al*, 2012).

- 'the ability to consistently produce near-perfect performance on a specific task' (Rath and Conchie, 2008).

- 'a pre-existing capacity for a particular way of behaving, thinking or feeling that is authentic and energizing to the user, and enables optimal functioning, development and performance' (Linley, 2008).

- 'a capacity for feeling, thinking, and behaving in a way that allows optimal functioning in the pursuit of valued outcomes' (Snyder, Lopez and Pedrotti, 2010).

- 'a personal characteristic or quality that makes you feel energized and enthusiastic and leads you to doing great work' (Brewerton and Brook, 2010).

From these definitions, we can see that strengths can be variously defined as traits, abilities, capacities and qualities (see Figure 2.1). Crucially all definitions make some link to performance whereas only some indicate a link to a positive motivational state. There is, however, almost no explicit speculation in these definitions on the origin of strengths. Implicitly at least traits have the flavour of

FIGURE 2.1   Strengths across the state–trait continuum

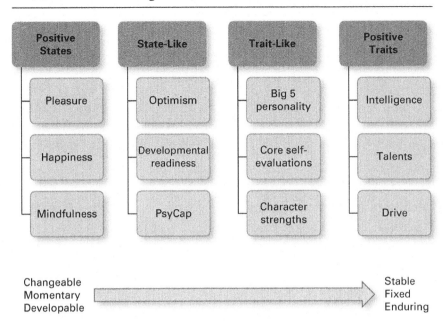

long-standing (possibly inherited) dispositions, whereas abilities have the perception of being able to be acquired by effort and deliberate practice. While it is not yet possible to be definitive about the origins of strengths, we can say with some certainty that the beliefs you hold about your own strengths go a long way to determining what you do with them. Thus, a fixed mindset around strengths leads inevitably to a focus on identification of strengths, whereas a growth mindset leads more to a development orientation (Dweck, 2006). We shall return to the importance of mindsets in Chapter 3.

Models of strengths

There are a variety of models of strengths, each informed by differing theoretical perspectives. Acknowledging the origin of the model is important as it usually has implications for how the model is applied and interpreted in the leadership development setting. It is no surprise to find that some of the traditional dichotomies in psychology, eg state versus trait, are manifest in the definitions and models of extant strength-based approaches. Existing models can be broadly classified into domain-based models, capacity-based models and character- or trait-based models.

Domain–based models of strengths

Domain-based models usually start with some exploratory research or conceptual thinking that suggest that individual strengths can be sensibly grouped under the relevant domain headings. A good example of this is the Gallup Strengthsfinder (see Chapter 4) which lists 34 strengths under the four leadership domains of executing, influencing, relationship building and strategic thinking. Other models combine trait- and domain-based approaches. Domains serve several functions in that they can combine large amounts of strengths (up to 60 in the case of the Realise2 inventory described in Chapter 4) into a much more manageable set of constructs, usually around five. Domains are usually positioned as heuristics that provide broad indications of areas of strength and development but don't necessarily have the underlying statistical validity that the individual strengths tend to display. These approaches are similar to competency-based approaches that have been around in human resource management for some time.

Capacity-based models of strengths

Other models emphasize the latent capacity of individuals to perform well in particular areas. This is achieved by either tapping into a pre-existing positive motivational affect or by cultivating positive emotions that provide the ability to lead others more effectively through enhanced engagement. These models are usually more state or state-like in their appearance. The Realise2 model (Linley and Stoker, 2012) is a good example of the first approach where energy plus performance can equate to either a realized or unrealized strength depending on the opportunity for utilization. The psychological capital model (PsyCap (Avolio and Luthans, 2006)) is another illustrative example of the capacity model. PsyCap asserts that four state-like structures sit underneath the PsyCap domain, namely hope, optimism, self-efficacy and resilience. These four structures share a common link in that they all impact on an individual's motivational propensity to achieve goals. The PsyCap model differs from other strength models in that it is much more circumscribed (1 domain and 4 constructs), demonstrates good reliability and validity, is explicitly state-like and has been proven to be easily developed with specific interventions (Luthans *et al*, 2006). There is also evidence that these states are positively impacted on by positive leadership behaviours and that, in turn, an increase in the PsyCap propensities in the follower results in enhanced workplace performance, extra effort and improved satisfaction (see Chapter 3 for a further elaboration of this link).

Another interesting state-like model of strengths that has particular relevance to leadership development is the concept of developmental readiness (Hannah and Avolio, 2010). This construct attempts to identify the essential capacities that precede learning and development activities, namely the motivation and ability to change, grow and develop. Developmental readiness is to some degree predicated on an accurate self-appraisal of strengths as well as a strong commitment to the change process. It is something rarely assessed prior to coaching interventions but actually predicts who will benefit from such experiences (MacKie, 2015).

Trait-based models of strengths

Trait-based approaches to strengths can include standard models of personality like the Big 5 (stability, extraversion, openness, agreeableness and conscientiousness), core self-evaluations that include self-esteem, confidence, locus of control and emotional stability (Judge and Bono, 2001) and character strengths. Character-based strength models bring a crucial ingredient to the modelling of strengths, a moral perspective. While many models in coaching shy away from making explicit judgements about the moral equivalence of strengths, character strength models make the link to virtues explicit. The Values in Action (VIA) model is an illustrative example of this where strengths are seen as derivatives of virtues and therefore have embedded values in them. Values appear in several models of leadership, including transformational leadership, and have been proposed as the foundation on which transformational elements of leadership sit (Avolio, 2010). Another interesting example of the trait approach is the Gallup model of talent (Hodges and Asplund, 2010). Although this approach has elements of the domain approach above it also incorporates the notion of 'natural' talents that, with the application of deliberate practice and utilization, can be transformed into strengths. This is very much an 'entity' theory of talent that has its own implications for development (see Chapter 3).

Standard models of personality like the Big 5 also offer opportunities to identify more enduring and stable strengths in the individual. Personality, by definition, describes traits that are relatively constant over time and tend to be easily discernible by an observer. Some personality traits, especially extraversion consistently provide small but significant correlations with leadership behaviour (Judge *et al*, 2002). The core skill in utilizing personality-based models to reveal strengths is to consider the fit with the individual's role and their underlying preferences. The challenge with trait-based models is that they are identifying elements of character which, by definition, are long-standing and enduring elements of personality and are therefore not ideal targets for executive and leadership development.

Process models

Process models of strengths outline a pathway for their application and inclusion without making too many definitive statements about their origin. Appreciative inquiry (AI) is a good example of a model that prescribes such a process but with more emphasis on organizational than individual change (Cooperrider and Sekerka, 2006). The AI process sees strengths identification within individuals as the first stage in organizational development. Strengths then need to be shared amongst others to leverage the combinatorial effect before the organization can really benefit.

Strength model summary

The majority of models are agnostic on the origins of strengths but may allude to predispositions, talents and preferences that shape the individual's presenting strengths. It is useful to grade these models along the state–trait continuum from positive states like happiness at one end to traits like intelligence at the other (see Figure 2.1). Each model has implications for the subsequent development of the strength concerned so it is important to be aware of these prior to selecting an approach in strength-based leadership coaching.

Differentiating strengths across the state–trait continuum

The different models illustrated above give the impression that not all strengths are the same in terms of their capacity for development. This difference in flexibility has been traditionally captured in psychology across the state–trait continuum. This continuum suggests that strengths identified and developed from the positive states and state-like end of the continuum have a much better capacity for development than those selected from the trait end which have traditionally been seen as more stable and enduring. Indeed, the perception of the fixity of the strength has to some extent driven the consequent methodology with character strengths more associated with the 'identify and use' approach. So is this continuum still supported by the evidence? As a heuristic for strength selection it has value in that it does illustrate an important trend in strengths research in terms of relative flexibility of states versus traits. However, there is also evidence to suggest that the malleability of trait-like constructs has been underestimated and that this mindset contains within it self-limiting beliefs that are significant in their capacity to inhibit change. In other words, the beliefs you hold about the changeability of your strengths may be as or more important in determining the capacity for change than the nature of the strengths themselves (see box overleaf).

This state–trait continuum model suggests that positive states like happiness are relatively easy to acquire but lack the permanence and stability required for an effective strength. The state-like strengths including developmental readiness and PsyCap are much more trainable and have direct impacts on leadership effectiveness. Personality traits and character strengths are by definition more enduring but by no means fixed. One illustrative example of this is the effectiveness of therapeutic interventions like mindfulness on disorders of low adjustment like anxiety. Finally, positive traits like intelligence and other talents have traditionally been perceived with an entity mindset, but that is changing as evidence accumulates from epigenetics, the Flynn effect and the absence of identification of genes for intelligence. These concepts are further expanded in the box below.

How flexible is intelligence?

If strengths are arranged across a state–trait continuum, a real challenge for the approach is the extent to which strengths that fall in the trait end of the continuum can be modified. Take intelligence as an example of a strength that most people would desire to enhance. The majority of people subscribe implicitly or explicitly to an entity theory of intelligence. This perspective has been largely supported by the psychology profession over the years through genetic and twin studies, the reification of intelligence into an IQ score and its apparent stability over time and lifespan (Deary, 2001). However, less well known is the unravelling that has occurred in the entity model since the advent of the human genome project and the almost total failure to reliably identify genes for intelligence that explain or predict a significant proportion of an individual's intellectual capacity. A recent study of over 100,000 people (Rietveld *et al*, 2013) investigated the genes that may be linked to intelligence. They found that of the three genes located with links to both educational attainment and higher IQ scores, these genes each accounted for only about 0.3 points on a standard IQ team (where the average score is 100). By contrast the effects for genes on height are about 20 times stronger.

Compare this to the work on mindsets by Carol Dweck (2006). In her landmark studies she measured growth and fixed mindsets about intellectual capacity in adolescent school children and then measured the impact on their grades over two years. Those with a fixed mindset declined in their maths grades, while those with a growth scored significantly better. She then taught the growth model to those with implicit fixed theories and reversed the effects in eight weeks. So mindsets matter more than genes in this case (although the two could be connected) and mindsets can be changed and developed, significantly boosting scholastic achievement.

Finally, the research programme of James Flynn (2007) provides compelling evidence for the malleability at least in the measurement of intelligence. Flynn documented a rise in IQ scores of nearly 14 points (or 14 per cent as the mean IQ score is 100) over a 50-year period. Flynn attributed this rise to largely environmental factors, growing up in an increasingly more stimulating environment and this effect is now known eponymously as the Flynn effect. Compare the strength of the Flynn effect to the 0.3 IQ point attributed to the genes for intelligence discussed above.

The strengths and performance link

Strengths are of interest to us in the first place because of their apparent capacity to enhance the development and performance of individuals in the workplace. How strengths relate to leadership performance has also generated a significant amount of research in the field of positive organizational psychology. If we agree there is a relationship, the most common options are a positive correlation, a negative correlation or a curvilinear relationship (see Figure 2.2). A positive correlation would mean that increasing strength utilization always increases leadership performance, whereas for a negative correlation, the converse would be true. The curvilinear relationship suggests there is

FIGURE 2.2   Curvilinear relationship between confidence and performance

an optimum titration of strengths, beyond which leadership performance would decline. There is now a consensus emerging that the relationship is predictably curvilinear rather than linear with strengths following a classic inverted U shape in their relationship with performance (Kaiser and Overfield, 2010). The evidence for this comes from a variety of sources, including the derailment literature which examines the reasons why individuals fail to achieve their expected career potential, and from the literature that examines the links between specific personality traits and performance. All strengths can be overdone where, for example, confidence can lead to arrogance or inclusive decision-making can develop into procrastination.

Evidence from leadership derailment studies

The leadership derailment literature shows that when overdone strengths become weaknesses, and this can be in the form of excessive leverage or contextual misapplication. Thus, a leader with a well-developed strength for inclusivity can persist with this beyond the point of additional value or apply this to a situation that requires a more urgent and directive response (Kaiser, 2009). This over-application of strengths has been termed 'lopsided' leadership.

Evidence from personality studies

The research on the relationship between personality and job performance has also recently demonstrated convincing evidence for a curvilinear relationship (Le *et al*, 2011). Research looking at a variety of personality variables and task performance found that for variables such as conscientiousness and emotional stability there was a clear curvilinear relationship between the two variables. This makes sense if you think about how conscientiousness can manifest as indecisiveness when exaggerated or emotional stability can eventually appear as disinterest. Confirmation of this connection has come from data looking specifically at the relationship between assertiveness and leadership (Ames and Flynn, 2007). Moderate levels of assertiveness clearly facilitate the achievements of outcomes but high levels undermine the quality of the interpersonal relationship making achieving through others challenging.

Evidence for the nonmonotonic connection between personality variables and performance has also been found in teams. Not surprisingly, teams can have too many extraverts causing the balance between people and task focus to tilt in favour of social engagement. Performance then diminishes as a consequence (Barry and Stewart, 1997). This impact on strengths at the team levels reminds us of the importance of complementary strengths both within and between individuals.

Evidence from studies on positive emotion

Recent research in positive organizational behaviour has also investigated the impacts of positive emotion on performance (Lam, Spreitzer and Fritz, 2013). Given that positive emotion is both an element and product of transformational leadership and often the target of workplace coaching interventions, understanding its impact on performance criteria is a crucial step. Intuitively, positive emotions appear to be linked to performance, in that those who experience greater optimism, confidence and hope would persist longer with goals, offer more discretionary effort and recover more quickly from setbacks. Positive emotions have also been linked to increased proactive behaviours where individuals take the initiative, anticipate customer needs and form better relationships with their managers. Proactive behaviours have also been hypothesized to be mediated by individuals using affect as information – that is, if it feels like I can achieve this goal, I probably can. The relationship between positive emotion and proactivity has also been found to be curvilinear, indicating again that it is possible to have too much of a good thing. One explanation is that when positive emotions are high things are perceived to be going well, which reduces the need for more proactivity. Similarly, a recent meta-analysis showed that the relationship between positive emotion and creativity was also nonmonotonic, instead taking the shape of an inverted U (Davis, 2008). Excessive optimism too has its downside with high optimism leading to poor preparation and the underestimation of risk (Grant and Schwartz, 2011). High levels of optimism and satisfaction can inhibit the dissatisfaction that can motivate individuals to change and develop. Too much positivity can feel vacuous and insincere, drowning developmental feedback in a wave of Pollyanna-like rhetoric.

In 2005 an influential paper was published (Fredrickson and Losada, 2005) that suggested there were ideal ratios of positivity within teams and, by inference, individuals and organizations. They suggested that high performing teams had a positivity ratio of about 5:1 – that is five positive comments for every negative.

However, this research has been recently challenged and it seems more likely the ideal ratio is around 3:1. Nonetheless, this data does confirm yet another curvilinear relationship with performance, indicating that too much or too little positivity can have an adverse impact on performance. See the box on positivity ratio controversy on page 168 in Chapter 9 for further discussion on this topic.

The collective evidence from studies on derailment, personality and positive emotion all support the notion of the curvilinear relationship between variables that can be conceived of as strengths and a variety of performance criteria. Given that many strengths are defined as traits like constructs, it would be reasonable to assume that by analogy the same relationship would hold for strengths and aspects of workplace performance. This research gives an unambiguous direction on how strengths might be developed and strongly suggests that the unregulated leverage of strengths, independent of intensity or context, will adversely impact on performance (Kaiser and Overfield, 2011).

Strengths overdone

The above research suggests that strengths overdone can become derailers for the individual. We will dig deeper into the challenges of the strength-based approach in Chapter 10, but for now it is worth remembering that adopting a strength-based approach does not mean that weaknesses are ignored or strengths are applied without due consideration to context and amplitude. Much of the research in positive psychology has been focused on the adverse impacts of the absence of strength-based behaviour rather than the dangers of excessive leverage of strengths (Grant and Schwartz, 2011). There are a number of models that illustrate how strengths can be overdone. The inverted U model mentioned above clearly illustrates what happens to performance when strengths are amplified in an unregulated way. Narcissism is a great example of this, where confidence and self-belief can all too quickly become hubris and arrogance.

Other models of overuse include lopsided leadership (Kaplan and Kaiser, 2013) where overuse is seen as a function of lack of versatility, whereby leaders fail to balance their behaviour along key dimensions of strategic versus operational and forceful versus enabling leadership. However, this model assumes that balance needs to occur within the individual rather than more broadly within the team or organization (Linley *et al*, 2010).

Strengths in context

Applied psychology has wrestled with a number of ingrained dichotomies, none more apparent than the emphasis on personal traits versus environmental influence. Of course, this is a false dichotomy – success requires both traits and environment – but how do they interact? Personality traits are a good example of how to consider the interaction of traits and environment. Personality traits tend to show a correlational ceiling with leadership and performance criteria, probably due to the curvilinear association outlined above. Although extraversion, for example, consistently shows a positive correlation with some leadership behaviours, think about the context in which those traits may be either functional or inhibitory depending on the demands of the role. In sales, extraversion is a necessity as it gives people the energy to engage with customers and clients continuously, building rapport, dealing with setbacks and promoting products. Imagine, however, those same traits in an IT department where quiet reflection is the norm. How might those same traits ripple through such an environment? Clearly context is key here and strengths must be applied mindfully to match the demands of the situation and environment in which they are applied.

Strengths and decision latitude

This is another key contextual question in deciding if a strength-based approach will be helpful for your development. If you have a degree of choice as to how to deliver results in your role, then you have the flexibility to play around with various combinations of strengths in order to titrate optimal effectiveness. But what if you don't? Then it's more helpful to consider how the role fits with your strengths and, if there is a gap, how developable the gap is. Some roles do require specific skill sets, conscientious in a legal role, for example, and it would be draining and unrewarding to perform them if this approach is not a preference.

Summary and conclusion

At the beginning of this chapter I posed some questions around the construct of discriminant and predictive validity of the concept of strengths. So far the jury is still out on whether the construct of strengths is a new category of psychological phenomena. The state–trait continuum model incorporates many existing psychological constructs like emotions, personality traits and talents but uses them in a novel way to enhance performance. The evidence for the link between strengths and performance is much clearer. There is convergent evidence that this is curvilinear and it is consequently possible to have too much of a good thing. This finding has significant implications for how strengths are developed (see Chapter 5). Finally, the role of a growth mindset in adopting a strength-based approach is paramount. Despite strengths varying in their developability across the state–trait continuum, there is evidence that even traits like intelligence, that were assumed to be relatively fixed, have the capacity for development under the right conditions.

Some questions to consider

- What is your mindset in relation to growth and development?
- What are some of your beliefs about leadership and what is the evidence for them?
- When developing strengths do you tend to pick mainly states or traits to develop?
- When appraising others, do you consider their strengths and, if so, do they tend to be state-like or trait-like?

References

Ames, D R and Flynn, F J (2007) What breaks a leader: the curvilinear relation between assertiveness and leadership, *Journal of Personality and Social Psychology*, **92** (2), pp 307–24

Avolio, B J (ed) (2010) *Full Range Leadership Development*, SAGE Publications, Thousand Oaks, CA

Avolio, B J and Luthans, F (2006) *The High Impact Leader*, McGraw-Hill, New York

Barry, B and Stewart, G L (1997) Composition, process, and performance in self-managed groups: the role of personality, *Journal of Applied Psychology*, **82** (1), pp 62–78

Brewerton, P and Brook, J (2010) *Strengths for Success: Your pathway to peak performance*, Strengths Partnership Press, London

Cooperrider, D and Sekerka, L E (2006) Toward a theory of positive organizational change, *Organization Development: A Jossey-Bass Reader*, pp 223–38

Davis, M A (2009) Understanding the relationship between mood and creativity: a meta-analysis, *Organizational Behavior and Human Decision Processes*, **108** (1), pp 25–38

Deary, I J (2001) *Intelligence: A very short introduction*, Oxford University Press, Oxford

Dweck, C S (2006) *Mindset: The new psychology of success*, Random House, New York

Flynn, J R (2007) *What is Intelligence?: Beyond the Flynn effect*, Cambridge University Press

Fredrickson, B L and Losada, M F (2005) Positive affect and the complex dynamics of human flourishing, *American Psychologist*, **60** (7), pp 678–86

Grant, A M and Schwartz, B (2011) Too much of a good thing: the challenge and opportunity of the inverted U, *Perspectives on Psychological Science*, **6** (1), pp 61–76

Hannah, S T and Avolio, B J (2010) Ready or not: how do we accelerate the developmental readiness of leaders? *Journal of Organizational Behavior*, **31** (8), pp 1181–87

Hodges, T D and Asplund, J (2009) Strengths development in the workplace, *Oxford Handbook of Positive Psychology and Work*, pp 3–9

Judge, T A and Bono, J E (2001) Relationship of core self-evaluations traits – self-esteem, generalized self-efficacy, locus of control, and emotional stability – with job satisfaction and job performance: a meta-analysis, *Journal of Applied Psychology*, **86** (1), pp 80–92

Judge, T A *et al* (2002) Personality and leadership: a qualitative and quantitative review, *Journal of Applied Psychology*, **87** (4), pp 765–80

Kaiser, R B (ed) (2009) *The Perils of Accentuating the Positive*, Hogan Press, Tulsa, OK

Kaiser, R B and Overfield, D V (2010) Assessing flexible leadership as a mastery of opposites, *Consulting Psychology Journal: Practice and Research*, **62** (2), pp 105–18

Kaiser, R B and Overfield, D V (2011) Strengths, strengths overused, and lopsided leadership, *Consulting Psychology Journal: Practice and Research*, **63** (2), pp 89–109

Kaplan, R E and Kaiser, R B (2013) *Fear Your Strengths: What you are best at could be your biggest problem*, Berrett-Koehler, Oakland, CA

Lam, C F, Spreitzer, G and Fritz, C (2014) Too much of a good thing: curvilinear effect of positive affect on proactive behaviors, *Journal of Organizational Behavior*, **35** (4), pp 530–46

Le, *et al* (2011) Too much of a good thing: curvilinear relationships between personality traits and job performance, *Journal of Applied Psychology*, **96** (1), pp 113–33

Linley, P A (2008) *Average to A+: Realising strengths in yourself and others*, CAPP Press, Coventry

Linley, P A, Harrington, S and Garcea, N (2010) *Oxford Handbook of Positive Psychology and Work*, Oxford University Press, New York

Linley, P A and Stoker H (2012) *Technical Manual and Statistical Properties for Realise2*, Centre of Applied Positive Psychology, Coventry

Luthans, F *et al* (2006) Psychological capital development: toward a micro-intervention, *Journal of Organizational Behavior*, **27** (3), pp 387–93

MacKie, D (2015) The effects of coachee readiness and core self-evaluations on leadership coaching outcomes: a controlled trial, *Coaching: An International Journal of Theory, Research and Practice*, **8** (2), pp 120–36

Rath, T and Conchie, B (2008) *Strengths Based Leadership: Great leaders, teams, and why people follow,* Gallup Press, New York

Rietveld, *et al* (2013) GWAS of 126,559 individuals identifies genetic variants associated with educational attainment, *Science*, **340** (6139), pp 1467–71

Snyder, C R, Lopez, S J and Pedrotti, J T (2010) *Positive Psychology: The scientific and practical explorations of human strengths*, SAGE Publications, Thousand Oaks, CA

Zenger, J H *et al* (2012) *How to Be Exceptional: Drive leadership success by magnifying your strengths*, McGraw-Hill, New York

Positive leadership theories

03

CHAPTER OVERVIEW

This chapter covers:

- Origin and evolution of leadership theory
- Brief history of leadership – including transformational and authentic
- Implicit leadership theories
- Mindsets and developmental readiness
- How do strengths link to positive leadership?
- Positive global leadership
- Outcomes in positive leadership development

Introduction

This chapter introduces some of the positive leadership theories behind the strength-based approach. Looking at leadership theory provides us with the conceptual platform through which to reflect on our practice. It also provides us with coherent frameworks and hypotheses that can be tested in the applied setting. To understand a theory, it is necessary both to understand its origins and the context in which it developed. Leadership evolved for a reason and leadership theories too have developed over time in their attempts to explain leadership behaviour. Positive leadership is the most recent example of the evolution of models to help us understand and develop effective leadership practices.

The origin of leadership behaviour

It is worth reflecting on why leadership behaviour may have evolved in the first place and in what context. Most evolutionary psychologists take a functional approach to the evaluation of behaviours like leadership and speculate on the adaptive value that such behaviours may confer. If we consider our ancestors evolving in the African savanna around 200,000 years ago, what adaptive challenges did they face? Many of those critical challenges revolved around group cohesion and communal decision-making. Many animals used dominance hierarchies to coordinate groups but this is unlikely to have been the case in humans. In fact, almost the opposite has been documented with reverse dominance hierarchies ensuring that no leader became too powerful (Boehm, 1999). Many of our beliefs about leadership evolved in this environment of evolutionary adaptation and were not significantly challenged until farming and cities promoted more centralized, hierarchical and inherited leadership structures (van Vugt, Hogan and Kaiser, 2008). So despite business leadership being only around 250 years old, it maps onto much older evolutionary structures that have evolved over millennia. Modern leadership structures are, however, more complex in both the size of the groups they attempt to coordinate and the greater emphasis on persuasion in engaging followers who, after all, can and do leave to join other groups. Evolutionary models offer us the following insights into contemporary leadership. They suggest evolved propensities for distributed leadership and egalitarian structures. They promote the concept of flexible leadership in response to different environmental challenges. Finally, they suggest leadership styles change as a function of social complexity and group size.

Leadership theory too has also evolved, especially in the last 100 years from 'great man' to more transformational, distributed and authentic models. The multiple theories of leadership often aim to explain different elements of the leadership process, but all have embedded and implicit assumptions. Great man theories evolved at a time when history provided multiple examples of charismatic individuals who seem to have been born to lead. Hence, much of the leadership research at that time focused on unpacking the leadership qualities required to lead successfully. Implicit in this model was the assumption that these traits were born rather than acquired, so finding a leader became a process of selection rather than development. The difficulties of defining and developing the specific leadership qualities inherent in the great man hypothesis resulted in theories focusing more on the behaviours in leaders that could be learned and developed. Behaviourist and situational theories added another layer of complexity in that they introduced the importance of both the follower and the context within which leadership emerged. The first positive model of leadership arrived in the form of transformational leadership that suggested extra discretionary effort could be unlocked from the follower by focusing on the augmentation effect derived from inspiring others towards a higher collective purpose. Hence, positive theories of leadership and its development are relatively new but build on a long history of research focused on leaders, followers and the process between them. We will now look at some of the existing models of positive leadership in more detail.

Positive leadership theories

In order to be classified as a positive leadership, explicit theories need several elements. Firstly, there needs to be a focus on the strengths, on what's outstanding and constructive in the leader. Secondly, there needs to be a positive impact on followers, both in terms of their individual capability, eg confidence or self-efficacy, and in terms of their performance output. Finally, the purpose of the positive leadership theory has to be self-transcendent, that is, in service of a purpose that is beyond the self-interest of the individual leader.

Positive leadership theories can be either explicit, eg those formally adopted in a leadership development process, or implicit, that is, those embedded in the underlying assumptions and behaviours of the organization and its leadership practices. Implicit leadership theories are crucial as, in part, they determine the organizations' and the individuals' readiness to change and develop as a leader. Thus, implicit leadership theories (ILTs) are moderators of the development of positive leadership behaviours. Leaders who are not ready or able to change, or who have a fixed mindset about their own leadership development, will struggle to engage with positive leadership development programmes.

Implicit leadership theories

Implicit leadership theories are important as they mediate beliefs about the performance and potential of both the leader and those they appraise (Heslin and Vandewalle, 2008). There are two major implicit theories of leadership that are worthy of exploration: mindsets (Dweck, 2006) and developmental readiness (Avolio and Hannah, 2008).

Mindsets

Mindsets are based on trying to understand factors behind achievement motivation. Why is it that some people seem to excel at developing themselves, acquiring new skills and performing in academic environments whilst others struggle? Why are some individuals so positive when faced with learning challenges whilst others move away from such opportunities? The traditional answer was 'intelligence' or capability (but see the 'How flexible is intelligence?' box in Chapter 2 at page 32 for a refutation of this belief), but several factors including the carefully controlled studies of Dweck and others have seriously challenged this belief. The original research was based on the impact of growth versus fixed mindsets on scholastic achievements. The conclusions were that mindsets matter, growth mindsets boost scholastic achievement and fixed mindsets do the opposite. Mindsets can be changed and growth mindsets acquired in a short period of time. So the mindset of the coachee towards their learning and development predict to some degree the effectiveness of that development. In addition, the mindsets of their managers matter too in that these beliefs moderate performance ratings and coaching behaviour in the manager (Heslin and Vandewalle, 2008). This work has recently been extended to the field of talent management where beliefs about the scarcity, developability and origins of talent predict how talent is recruited, assessed and developed within organizations (Meyers and van Woerkom, 2014). Recent developments in leadership theory, like distributed or shared leadership, are predicated on the understanding that talent is more widely distributed than previously thought.

Developmental readiness

The other key implicit leadership theory is developmental readiness. Developmental readiness has been defined as 'both the ability and the motivation to focus on, make meaning of and develop new and more complex ways of thinking that position you to more effectively assume leadership roles' (Avolio and Hannah, 2008). It's a critical precursor to positive leadership development as it attempts to identify key positive states and traits within the leader that signal a readiness to constructively and effectively engage in a leadership development process. These elements include the ability to change, including self-awareness, self-regulation, clarity around the type of leader they wanted to become, and a capacity to reflect on their own cognition. The motivation to change was also seen as critical, with elements including self-confidence, goal setting and intrinsic interests.

My own research on developmental readiness (MacKie, 2015) in coaching investigated the impact of coachee readiness for change and core personality traits as both criteria and predictors of outcomes after strength-based leadership coaching. Specifically, this study examined developmental readiness, change readiness in the coachee to measure both their capacity to predict changes in transformational leadership and to act as outcome criteria in themselves after coaching. Thirty executives and senior managers from a large not-for-profit organization were assigned to either a coaching or waitlist cohort using a between-subjects control group design. The coaching group received six sessions of leadership coaching involving feedback on leadership and strengths, goal setting and strengths development. The results showed that participants in the waitlist first group declined in both developmental and coaching readiness whilst waiting for coaching. Change readiness at the start of the research programme for the group who had their coaching first was a significant predictor of enhanced leadership effectiveness after coaching. The results suggest that these coachee variables are both outcome criteria and predictors of change after leadership coaching.

Explicit positive leadership theories

Explicit leadership theories are those that are formally adopted as models and methods to facilitate positive leadership development in organizations. They include transformational, authentic, servant and global leadership.

Transformational leadership

Transformational leadership emphasized the leader's impact on their followers in terms of inspiring them towards enhancing their performance towards a shared vision for the benefit of the organization and its values (Bass, 1999). Bass integrated the five transformative elements of leadership into his full range leadership model (FRLM) that, in addition, included two transactional elements that focused on rewarding followers' behaviours and two laissez-faire elements that described the less functional passive and avoidant leadership styles (see box opposite). The model attained its psychometric manifestation in the Multifactor Leadership Questionnaire (MLQ (Bass and Avolio, 1997)). There is now a substantial amount of evidence supporting the construct validity of the FRLM, and the MLQ is one of the most commonly used leadership instruments by both researchers and practitioners in the field (Alban-Metcalfe and Mead, 2010). It has also been the inspiration for several psychometrics that attempt to capture the construct that will be reviewed in Chapter 4.

What is transformational leadership?

The five elements of transformational leadership sit within the nine elements of the full range leadership model (FRLM). These transformational elements are:

- idealized influence attributes or building trust with others (eg display a sense of power and confidence);

- idealized influence behaviour or acting with integrity (eg talk about my most important values and beliefs);

- inspirational motivation or inspiring others (eg articulate a compelling vision of the future);

- intellectual stimulation or encouraging innovation (eg seek different perspectives when solving problems);

- individualized consideration or helping to coach and develop others (eg help others to develop their strengths).

The two elements of transactional leadership in the model are contingent reward or rewards achievement (eg provide others with assistance in exchange for their efforts) and management by exception active or monitors mistakes (eg keep track of all mistakes). Finally, the two elements of the passive and avoidant elements of the model are management by exception passive or fights fires (eg fail to interfere until things become serious) and laissez-faire or avoids involvement (eg avoid making decisions).

Although the FRLM is the most common and researched transformational model, other models have identified and measured similar constructs. The Leadership Challenge (Kouzes and Posner, 2006) also identified five transformational leadership constructs, several of which bear a strong similarity to the five elements of transformational leadership in the FRLM. This model was subsequently developed into a psychometric (The Leadership Practices Inventory (LPI)) that is discussed in more detail in Chapter 4. However, it lacks the transactional and passive/avoidant elements of the model so the dark side of leadership is not articulated.

How do strengths link to transformational leadership?

It is worth reflecting on the potential mechanisms of transmission from increasing a leader's awareness and utilization of their strengths to others rating them higher on transformational leadership (TL) behaviours. There has been significant modelling done on how enhanced leadership may impact on team and organizational outcomes via the empowerment and engagement of followers (Barling, 2014) but relatively less has been done on the mechanisms whereby leadership training and coaching leads to enhanced leadership effectiveness in the first place. In my own research on strength-based leadership coaching, I used transformational leadership (TL) as the dependent variable and found significant changes in TL after only three months of strength-based coaching, in the perceptions of the followers of the coachee. Consequently, it is worth speculating on how a strength-based approach might have moderated or even mediated this relationship (see Figure 3.1). There are some clear potential linkages between the five elements of transformational leadership and strength-based approaches. For example, in the idealized influence domain of transformational leadership, leaders are attempting to influence followers positively with their capacity for building trusted relationships and their capacity for acting

FIGURE 3.1 Potential strengths embedded in each of the five domains of transformational leadership

Idealized Influence–Attributes (Building Trust)	• Increased confidence through strengths awareness • Authentic leadership – relational transparency
Idealized Influence–Behaviours (Acting with Integrity)	• Identify and leverage strengths in self and others • Ethical application/generative values, eg altruism
Inspirational Motivation (Inspiring Others to Achieve)	• Expression and engagement with positive emotions • Strengths alignment with vision and goals
Intellectual Stimulation (Encouraging Innovation)	• Balanced decision-making and problem-solving • Broaden and build responses through self-regulation
Individualized Consideration (Coaching and Developing Followers)	• Strength-based coaching for followers • Complementary pairing and strengths utilization

ethically and with integrity. These behaviours promote openness and transparency in relationships with others that are the foundation for effectively engaging and influencing followers. Equally, in the inspiring others domain, much of the language is around positive emotion which, as we have already seen, increases as a function of engaging with your strengths and aligning them with your vision and goals.

Psychological capital

Recall that in Chapter 2 we examined psychological capital as a state-like concept. Psychological capital or PsyCap also offers us another model of how transformational leadership can build strengths in others. PsyCap is defined as 'the positive appraisal of circumstances and probability for success based on motivated effort and perseverance' (Luthans *et al*, 2007). Underneath this higher order construct of PsyCap sit four state-like constructs of hope, optimism, self-efficacy and resilience. Being optimistic and hopeful about the future and confident in your future success and in your capacity to bounce back from adversity are clearly positive psychological states. Logically, having a reservoir of such states should lead to greater well-being and achievement, but how do these states link to performance in general and leadership performance in particular?

In terms of predicting objective work performance (that is measured by an independent rater rather than self-reported), PsyCap does correlate with both other-rated performance and job satisfaction. What is more, PsyCap can clearly be developed, with a number of training interventions demonstrating significant improvements in PsyCap (Avey *et al*, 2011). This is a positive start as we are interested in leveraging positive states like confidence or self-efficacy in the pursuit of greater workplace performance, but can this construct also enhance leadership effectiveness? Recalling some key aspects of transformational leadership, inspiring others is largely based around the cultivation of positive emotional states within followers. So do transformational leaderships build PsyCap in their followers?

The answer from current research appears to be yes. There is converging evidence that PsyCap mediates the impact of transformational leadership on follower performance (Gooty *et al*, 2009). That is when transformational leaders engage their followers in an inspiring and motivational way; this builds hope, optimism, confidence and resilience in their followers. This in turn unlocks the extra discretionary effort in followers that can enhance follower performance and improve output. So we have here a clear and evidence-based mechanism whereby enhancing transformational leadership can build the motivational capacity in followers to persist and engage with goal-orientated behaviour. When we consider the individual components of PsyCap as state-like strengths, this demonstrates how transformational leadership enhances performance through the cultivation of strengths in followers (see Figure 3.2). Notice in Figure 3.2 that transformational leadership is mediated by enhanced PsyCap in the followers which results in enhanced leadership outcomes including extra discretionary effort. This is then hypothesized to form a positive feedback loop to the leader creating a virtuous cycle of positive leadership development.

FIGURE 3.2 The relationship between transformational leadership, follower PsyCap and follower performance

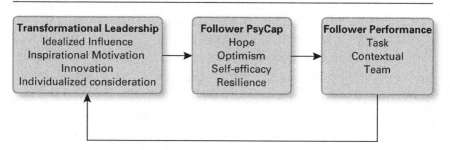

Authentic leadership

It is not surprising to find that leadership models reflect the genre they develop within. Authentic leadership gained traction in an era of corporate malfeasance and spectacular leadership derailments where the link between values and leadership had clearly been broken. This collective anxiety reached a peak in 2007 when numerous examples of poor decision-making and amoral behaviour, especially in the financial sector, led to the global financial crisis. Interest in authentic leadership blossomed in this crucible and led to a proliferation of models and constructs under this banner. Despite the proliferation of authentic leadership constructs at this time, all contained the core elements of transparency, ethical behaviour and the manifestation of positive and exemplary leader behaviour unconstrained by role. Many models of authentic leadership were also influenced by the positive organizational behaviour tradition and emphasized follower well-being, strengths development and the creation of a positive organizational context in their definitions (Gardner *et al*, 2011).

Authentic leadership also emerged out of the concept of transformational leadership when a distinction was made between manipulative and genuine transformational leaders (Barling, Christie and Turner, 2008). The concept of authentic leadership also capitalized on the increasing influence of positive organizational behaviour and offered a way to integrate this into a more strength-orientated leader development process. The model of authentic leadership defined by Luthans and Avolio (2003) as 'a process that draws from both positive psychological capacities and a highly developed organizational context which results in both greater self-awareness and self-regulated positive behaviours' appears to have gained the most empirical traction and has been operationalized into the Authentic Leadership Questionnaire (see Chapter 4). This model contained four key constructs: balanced processing in decision-making, an internalized moral perspective, relational transparency with others and self-awareness (Walumbwa *et al*, 2008). These four scales appeared to load onto a higher order factor of authenticity that was distinguishable from the concept of transformational leadership. Consequently the development of authentic leaders involves the identification and enhancement of positive psychological states and the integration of a moral element into leadership development to further develop the purpose as well as the process of leadership (Avolio and Gardner, 2005). While the ideal values of the authentic leader are rarely specified, there is a sense that these have to be self-transcendent, eg honesty or equality (Michie and Gooty, 2005).

So how important is authentic leadership? It has been suggested that this could be the 'root' cause of all forms of positive leadership (Avolio and Gardner, 2005). I think the sub-themes, especially around relational transparency, need to be further developed for this to be the case. Whilst the emphasis on ethical decision-making is admirable, it's as yet unclear whether there can be too much authenticity in leader–follower relationships. In the same way that strengths overdone no longer become strengths (Niemiec, 2014), I think too much authenticity at the wrong time could adversely impact performance. There is also the power differential between leader and follower to be considered here (Tourish, 2013). I know of many leaders who are understandably cautious of speaking openly and directly in a climate of efficiency drives, cost reduction and capital restraint.

How do strengths link to authentic leadership?

Does the building of strengths in the leader lead directly to more positive and authentic leader behaviours? Again, the answer appears to be a qualified yes, depending partially on the strength concerned. Authentic leadership is closely aligned to the concept of psychological capital in that the goal of the authentic expression of beliefs and values is the elevation of trust, hope and optimism in their followers (Hernandez *et al*, 2011). The individual elements of authentic leadership can also be viewed as strengths to be developed but, partly because of the recency of its development, there is less empirical evidence for the performance impact of these elements than there is for other theories, eg transformational leadership.

Servant leadership

The core of servant leadership is the altruistic development of others and the internalization of self-transcendent values (Liden *et al*, 2008). Like authentic leadership, it emerged in the context of increasing corporate corruption and rampant self-interest, although its origins may be much older (Greenleaf, 1977). In addition to items also found in other models like transformational leadership, servant leadership emphasizes that positive impact on the community is an aspired outcome. It is the antithesis of the hubris and narcissism that was thought to predicate much of the corporate dysfunction apparent in the global financial crisis, emphasizing self-sacrifice and subordinate well-being. Servant leadership aligns well with other models like Level 5 leadership (Collins, 2006) that emphasize leader humility as core leadership characteristics, but there is to date little empirical evidence on its effectiveness in a corporate context.

Positive global leadership

Given the scale and complexity of many businesses and the global span of many organizations, it's no surprise to find that cross-cultural research has been attempting to identify the universal strengths common in global leaders (Youssef and Luthans, 2012). Positive global leadership has been defined as 'the systematic and integrated manifestation of leadership traits, processes, intentional behaviours and performance outcomes that are elevating, exceptional and affirmatory of the strengths, capabilities and development potential of leaders, their followers and their organizations over time and across cultures' (Youssef and Luthans, 2012). Thus, the model expands on existing theories of positive leadership traits and authentic and transformational behaviours, but does so in a global, cross-cultural context. Positive global leadership has the additional challenges of leading across geographical distance, across diverse and varied cultures and differing mindsets when it comes to ethics, values and success criteria. Despite the recency of this conceptual model, there is evidence that existing concepts like PsyCap will transfer readily to this broad and integrative approach (Story, 2011).

Outcomes in positive leadership development

It is worth reflecting on what outcomes are desired in strength-based and other forms of positive leader development. Traditionally the leadership outcome research has focused on individual leader-focused knowledge, skills and attitudes (KSAs) rather than the leader–follower process at the dyadic or even team levels (DeRue and Myers, 2014). So results can potentially be experienced at the behavioural, motivational and cognitive levels and these changes can be seen within individuals, pairs and groups. Strength-based approaches lend themselves to an individual and behavioural/motivational level of analysis, but increasingly these leadership effects are being found to ripple out beyond the specific leader to their teams, colleagues, and direct reports (MacKie, 2015). At the cognitive level, there is some interesting research on implicit leadership theories (ILTs). These are the beliefs that sit below the threshold of awareness about what attributes and behaviours make an effective leader in a given organization. A common ILT I hear repeatedly in organizations is that of the 'natural leader', that rare breed that through talent and inherited gifts just is effective in the leadership domain, no training necessary. The impact of ILTs is important as, if people uncritically adopt these, it may and does stop very able candidates with significant leadership potential from applying for leadership roles. It can also mean that high potential individuals are screened out of any succession or promotional process due to the ILTs of the appraising talent management panel. Making these beliefs explicit and checking their alignment with the evidence base is rarely a specific outcome of leadership interventions but is often a useful unintended consequence.

As new theories of positive leadership emerge, attempts have been made to integrate them into the numerous extant theories of leadership (Hernandez *et al*, 2011). In a review of multiple leadership theories, Hernandez *et al* looked at both the loci of leadership (that is, where leadership comes from) and the mechanism of transmission to others. This has evolved into a two-dimensional framework that maps leadership theories onto five loci and four potential mechanisms of transmission. Strengths as a construct most logically fit in the leader loci and rely on trait-based methods of transmission, whereas transformational leadership sits more in the dyadic loci and spans trait, behavioural, cognitive and affective methods of transmission. While the framework omits motivation as a key mechanism of transmission and has yet to integrate emerging models of team leadership (eg Hawkins, 2011), it provides a coherent framework for mapping core elements of leadership theories and more importantly provides a mechanism for the synthesis of positive states and traits into existing leadership theory.

Summary and conclusion

So how can positive leadership theories assist in the development of leadership strengths in the coachee and their followers? Firstly, theory matters – it provides direction for research, algorithms for assessment and frameworks for coaching. Implicit theories matter even more. Secondly, understanding the coach's, the coachee's and the organizational beliefs about leadership is essential in developing leadership skills. Finally, they provide dependent variables – that is, possible outcome areas to assess after strength-based leadership coaching. Many theories offer the framework for innovating new models of leadership that can then be tested empirically and inform evidence-based practice.

Some questions to consider

- Which positive leadership theories align with your practice and client group?
- Do the sub-components of positive leadership theories, like inspiring others or relational transparency, provide useful frameworks to assess your coaching clients?
- How might positive leadership theories help you design positive leadership development?
- Are the strengths embedded in positive leadership models state-like or trait-like?
- What are the implicit leadership theories in your organization and what influence do they have?

References

Alban-Metcalfe, J and Mead, G (2010) Coaching for transactional and transformational leadership, in *Leadership Coaching: Working with leaders to develop elite performance*, ed J Passmore, pp 211–28, Kogan Page, London

Avey, J B *et al* (2011) Meta-analysis of the impact of positive psychological capital on employee attitudes, behaviors, and performance, *Human Resource Development Quarterly*, **22** (2), pp 127–52

Avolio, B J and Gardner, W L (2005) Authentic leadership development: getting to the root of positive forms of leadership, *The Leadership Quarterly*, **16** (3), pp 315–38

Avolio, B J and Hannah, S T (2008) Developmental readiness: accelerating leader development, *Consulting Psychology Journal: Practice and Research,* **60** (4), pp 331–47

Barling, J (2014) *The Science of Leadership*, Oxford University Press, New York

Barling, J, Christie, A and Turner, N (2008) Pseudo-transformational leadership: towards the development and test of a model, *Journal of Business Ethics*, **81** (4), pp 851–61

Bass, B M (1999) Two decades of research and development in transformational leadership, *European Journal of Work and Organizational Psychology*, **8** (1), pp 9–32

Bass, B M and Avolio, B J (1997) *Full Range Leadership Development: Manual for the multifactor leadership questionnaire,* Mind Garden Inc, Palo Alto, CA

Boehm, C (1999) *Hierarchy in the Forest: The evolution of egalitarian behavior*, Harvard University Press, Cambridge, MA

Collins, J (2006) Level 5 leadership: the triumph of humility and fierce resolve, in *Managing Innovation and Change*, ed D Mayle, p 234, SAGE Publications, London

DeRue, D S and Myers, C G (2014) Leadership development: a review and agenda for future research, *The Oxford Handbook of Leadership and Organizations*, pp 829–52

Dweck, C S (2006) *Mindset: The new psychology of success*, Random House, New York

Gardner, W L *et al* (2011) Authentic leadership: a review of the literature and research agenda, *The Leadership Quarterly*, **22** (6), pp 1120–45

Gooty, J *et al* (2009) In the Eyes of the Beholder: transformational leadership, positive psychological capital, and performance, *Journal of Leadership and Organizational Studies*, **15** (4), pp 353–67

Greenleaf, R K (1977) *Servant Leadership*, Paulist Press, New York

Hawkins, P (2011) *Leadership Team Coaching: Developing collective transformational leadership*, Kogan Page, London

Hernandez, M *et al* (2011) The loci and mechanisms of leadership: exploring a more comprehensive view of leadership theory, *The Leadership Quarterly*, 22 (6), pp 1165–85

Heslin, P A and Vandewalle, D (2008) Managers' implicit assumptions about personnel, *Current Directions in Psychological Science*, 17 (3), pp 219–23

Kouzes, J M and Posner, B Z (2006) *The Leadership Challenge* (Vol. 3), John Wiley and Sons, Hoboken, NJ

Liden, R C *et al* (2008) Servant leadership: development of a multidimensional measure and multi-level assessment, *The Leadership Quarterly*, 19 (2), pp 161–77

Luthans, F and Avolio, B J (2003) Authentic leadership: a positive developmental approach, in *Positive Organizational Scholarship*, eds K S Cameron, J E Dutton and R E Quinn, pp 241–61, Berrett-Koehler, Oakland, CA

Luthans, F *et al* (2007) Positive psychological capital: measurement and relationship with performance and satisfaction, *Personnel Psychology*, 60 (3), pp 541–72

MacKie, D (2015) The effects of coachee readiness and core self-evaluations on leadership coaching outcomes: a controlled trial, *Coaching: An International Journal of Theory, Research and Practice*, 8 (2), pp 120–36

Meyers, M C and van Woerkom, M (2014) The influence of underlying philosophies on talent management: theory, implications for practice, and research agenda, *Journal of World Business*, 49 (2), pp 192–203

Michie, S and Gooty, J (2005) Values, emotions, and authenticity: will the real leader please stand up?, *The Leadership Quarterly*, 16 (3), pp 441–57

Niemiec, R M (2014) *Mindfulness and Character Strengths: A practical guide to flourishing*, Hogrefe Verlag, Göttingen

Story, J S (2011) A developmental approach to global leadership, *International Journal of Leadership Studies*, 6 (3), pp 375–89

Tourish, D (2013) The dark side of transformational leadership: a critical perspective, Routledge, Hove

Van Vugt, M, Hogan, R and Kaiser, R B (2008) Leadership, followership, and evolution: some lessons from the past, *American Psychologist*, 63 (3), pp 182–96

Walumbwa, F O *et al* (2008) Authentic leadership: development and validation of a theory-based measure, *Journal of Management*, 34, pp 89–126

Youssef, C M and Luthans, F (2012) Positive global leadership, *Journal of World Business*, 47 (4), pp 539–47

Strengths identification and assessment

04

CHAPTER OVERVIEW

This chapter covers:

- Types of data – psychometrics, interview, multi-rater
- The challenges of self-report data
- What is the value of psychometrics?
- Self-report questionnaires measuring strengths
- Multi-source feedback questionnaires
- Structured interview approaches to strength identification
- How assessment impacts on development

Introduction

Strengths assessment is a critical process in the strength-based coaching protocol. We have already seen in Chapter 2, that strengths come in a variety of formats including states, traits, domains and competencies and this diversity is reflected in the assessment measures that have been developed to date. Although the reliability and validity of these questionnaires is still developing, they add value to the strength-based coaching project in a number of ways. Firstly, they raise awareness in the individual as to where their strengths may lie. This is important as research suggests that many leaders have little awareness or insight into their strengths (Hill, 2001). Secondly, they provide a benchmark for the coachee to understand where they are at in terms of effectively using their strengths and allows them to track their progress over time. Thirdly, they provide a language and framework for the coaching process to discuss strengths and their utilization. Strengths assessment is in its early days and has not yet reached the level of independent verification that tests of personality, intelligence and leadership have achieved (Carlson *et al*, 2014). Nonetheless, it is worth reviewing the existing psychometrics to investigate what they have to offer in terms of facilitating the strengths assessment process.

What types of data can inform us about strengths?

There are a variety of types of data that can help elucidate individual strengths and, as we have already established, the type of data utilized has implications for the development process it catalyses. There are also some key data sources to consider in this process. Firstly, who do you ask? This may seem an obvious question, but consider the research on the reliability of self-reports (see box opposite on the challenges of self-report data). Self-report data is contingent on the self-awareness of the individual and yet it's the relative absence of this variable that often leads individuals into a coaching process in the first place. While one can never discount an individual's experience, its alignment with the perspectives of peers, colleagues and direct reports is crucial for that individual's success. Consequently a whole industry has developed around multi-rater or multi-source feedback (MSF) that attempts to deal with the challenges of self-report by pooling data from many sources. Thus, by combining many perspectives, the individual errors and variations in perspectives are balanced out and the wisdom of crowds becomes apparent. MSF is an intervention in itself and has the capacity to develop individuals on its own without any other input. In addition, many multi-rater instruments with a leadership focus provide benchmarks on optimal leadership behaviours as well as the opportunity for qualitative commentary on both strengths and weaknesses.

A second key domain in strengths assessment is the type of inquiry into their strengths. This can be in structured psychometric format where a questionnaire with sufficient reliability and validity is given to the individual, usually revealing their top 3–5 strengths according to the model employed. Alternatively, a structured interview methodology can be used where rich, qualitative data around when the individual is performing at their best may reveal the underlying strengths that facilitate this level of performance. These two methodologies are often complementary, providing both quantitative and qualitative assessment data. Finally, strengths can be derived from multi-source leadership feedback inventories that don't explicitly target strengths but often provide a list of top and bottom items as rated by all others.

The challenges of self-report data

There is a significant body of research that suggests that individuals may consistently overrate their performance on a variety of tasks and that the discrepancy is at its greatest in individuals who are objectively rated as performing in the lowest quartile (Dunning *et al*, 2003). There are several biases that can operate during self-assessment, including leniency bias and confirmatory bias, where individuals are more generous and positively biased in their own self-appraisals than in their assessment of others, that may explain some of these discrepancies. This can lead to poor self–other alignment in 360-degree feedback.

There are several possible reasons why accurate self-assessment is challenging for some people. People who struggle with self-assessment frequently lack a well-developed capacity for meta-cognition – that is, their capacity to think about their thinking. Without that capacity to self-assess the evidence for a judgement about capability, it often comes down to an intuition about performance that is personally rather than externally referenced. As Charles Darwin noted 'ignorance more frequently begets confidence than does knowledge' (Darwin, 1871). In addition, those who don't seek and act on feedback on a regular basis, can maintain blindspots throughout their career. Consequently new constructs like developmental readiness (see Chapter 3) have been developed to assess who is ready to embark on development activities and a big part of this construct is self-awareness.

When to use self versus other ratings

It is a common assumption that multi-rater feedback is generally more valid when trying to elucidate an individual's strengths. However, there are some qualities and behaviours that have relatively low observability and can be better assessed through self-assessment. These include variables like anxiety and self-esteem (Spain, Eaton and Funder, 2000). However, for leadership behaviours, their perception by others is crucial as the goal of leadership is to have a direct impact on followers. In addition, these are behaviours – not internal personality preferences – but external behaviours, so their visibility and observability should be high. Other-ratings of leadership and performance have also demonstrated high validity when compared to external and more objective benchmarks like assessment centre ratings (Atkins and Wood, 2002). Consequently, they are the ideal way to both provide feedback and monitor change over time when building leadership capacity through a strength-based approach. However, there are some caveats to the use of MSF. They are designed to be used for developmental rather than selection purposes and work best in a positive culture where constructive feedback is routinely given so that individuals are not blindsided by critical and challenging feedback.

What value do psychometrics add?

There is substantial evidence that *some* psychometric tests are able to predict behaviour at a significantly higher level than more subjective assessments like interview data and graphology (Cook, 2009). I emphasize the *some* here, as there are key aspects of psychometrics that make a difference. Not all psychometrics are the same and the key differentiating factors are: *reliability* – that is, does the test measure the construct consistently over time?; and *validity* – that is, does the test predict anything meaningful? Reliability and validity are often in opposition. Take eye colour, for example. We can construct a test that can measure this with a high degree of accuracy, but what is its validity in predicting future work or leadership performance?

Reliability measures the capacity of the test to repeat the same measurement over time. It is usually measured by comparing two different administrations of a test over time or investigating how the different items in a test relate to each other. There are different forms of reliability including:

- *Test-retest reliability*: Administer the same test over time to the same people and then correlate the results. This is important in domains like personality or intelligence that are hypothesized to remain fairly stable over time.

- *Internal consistency reliability*: Previously known as split half reliability, this measures the degree to which the questions are measuring the same construct. Scores range from 0, where there is no relationship between questions and the underlying construct, to 1, where the questions are all aligned around the same construct. The scores are expressed in the form of Cronbach's alpha with acceptable reliability found at scores greater than 0.7.

- *Parallel forms reliability*: Administer two forms of the same test to the same subjects and test the correlation between the two scores.

Validity measures the test's capacity to measure the area of interest in a meaningful way. There are several forms of validity but the key domains are:

- *Construct validity*: does the test actually measure leadership or strengths in the way it suggests it does?

- *Criterion validity*: does the test predict anything meaningful in the work environment (usually performance criteria of some sort but can also be less desirable outcomes like turnover or absenteeism)?

Psychometric tests do add value when there is empirical evidence for their reliability and validity, and this evidence base needs time to develop. Those that develop normative samples also allow comparisons with potentially thousands of other individuals who have taken the same test. In the case of ability testing, this reference can be very useful in terms of ranking performance. In the case of personality testing, the results are more nuanced as different roles require differing levels of specific personality variables. In the case of strengths, because the construct varies from state to trait and because of the idiographic nature of the assessment, normative comparisons are harder to apply.

Self-report strength-based questionnaires

When reviewing the self-report questionnaires it's important to remember the key qualities of an effective psychometric. Consider the reliability of this test, ie does it actually measure strengths as a construct? Consider also its validity. What does this test predict and does it do this better than other existing tests like personality or ability tests? This incremental validity is important if we are going to make the case for strengths as a separate category, distinct from well-established constructs like personality or intelligence. The first thing to notice about existing strength-based psychometrics is that there aren't very many of them. This is partly a function of the relative novelty of the approach and partly a function of some creative disagreement in the nature of the strength construct. Those that have been developed measure different constructs, propose different models and utilize different scoring procedures, so cross survey comparisons are difficult. The two major types of scoring are ipsative, where the individual is faced with some forced choice items and the questionnaire produces their relative strengths with no external objective comparisons, and normative, where the individual is compared to a relevant pool of people who have previously taken the text. Remember also that the assessment model steers development in a particular direction, so consider this when selecting an instrument.

Gallup StrengthsFinder 2.0

The Gallup StrengthsFinder (Rath, 2007) builds on the concept in Chapter 2 that talent multiplied by effort equals strengths. This model found its psychometric manifestation in the Gallup StrengthsFinder (Rath and Conchie, 2008) which attempts to describe four domains of leadership, namely executing, influencing, relationship building and strategic thinking, which are themselves clusters of the thirty-four strengths identified in the StrengthsFinder instrument. Participants rate themselves on 177 pairs of items on a Likert scale (usually a five- or seven-point rating scale) and asked to indicate which one describes them best. Despite being assessed on all 34 strengths, subjective self-assessment routinely only produces a list of the participant's top five relative strengths. The challenge with this psychometric is that much of the research is published in-house with limited peer reviewed information about the psychometric qualities of the instrument available. In addition, the scoring is ipsative with no attempt to reference scores to a broader normative sample limiting the StrengthsFinder's utility as a dependent variable. Gallup's own technical data report test-retest reliabilities for the 34 strengths ranging between 0.52 and 0.79 (Asplund *et al*, 2007) suggesting some of the items have sizable amounts of measurement error. In addition, criterion-related validity investigations found some high correlations between individual strengths and aspects of the Big 5 personality variables, eg the strength discipline correlated with conscientiousness, suggesting this inventory is predicated on a trait model of strengths (Asplund *et al*, 2007).

The Values in Action (VIA) Survey

A contrasting approach has been taken by Peterson *et al* (2010) in the development of a model designed to assess and measure strength of character. The Values in Action (VIA) project was developed as a counterpart to the various attempts to classify psychiatric disorder and distress. A review of the world's most influential religious and philosophical texts by the authors of the inventory led to the identification of six domains (wisdom, courage, humanity, justice, temperance and transcendence), all underpinned by specific signature strengths. The VIA then aimed to identify 24 signature strengths from these domains, that individuals recognize and apply to achieve fulfilment. Again like the StrengthsFinder, the VIA depends on the veracity of the self-assessment to produce a relative ranking of the top five character strengths. In terms of the construct validity of character strengths identified in the VIA, the underlying factor structure has been challenged and there is evidence to suggest it more closely fits the Big 5 model of personality than a discrete construct of six independent virtues (MacDonald *et al*, 2008). This is perhaps unsurprising given its explicit focus on strengths as character traits. Unlike the Gallup StrengthsFinder, there is no overt connection between the VIA and leadership behaviour. However, there are some implicit links to leadership with character strengths like authenticity, teamwork and leadership identified in the assessment (Money, Hillenbrand and da Camara, 2008). The test-retest reliability of the VIA is >0.7 and the Cronbach alphas are also over 0.7 indicating a good degree of reliability (Linley *et al*, 2007).

The Realise2 inventory

The Realise2 inventory (Linley and Stoker, 2012) takes a broad approach to the process of strengths assessment by including development areas and relative weaknesses in the assessment. The Realise2 model requires participants to rate 60 attributes according to how energizing they find them, how competently and how frequently they use them. This is an online strengths assessment and development tool that assesses 60 different attributes or strengths in the individual (eg curiosity, authenticity, and action). Participants respond on a seven-point Likert scale for each attribute across three dimensions of energy, performance and use. The responses are then classified into realized strengths, unrealized strengths, learned behaviours and weaknesses (Linley *et al*, 2010). The mean reliability scores across all 60 attribute item groupings was 0.82 (Linley and Stoker, 2012). Criterion validities with individual strengths include action and the work engagement scale (0.41).

The model then divides the responses into four quadrants: realized strengths that are known and used, unrealized strengths that are known but underutilized, learned behaviours where performance has been acquired but is not energizing, and weaknesses where both competence and energy are low. According to the model, the greatest developmental opportunity is found in unrealized strengths as these are underutilized areas of interest and competence. This approach differs from the VIA and StrengthsFinder in that it explicitly addresses the issue of weaknesses and strives to make them irrelevant, rather than ignoring them in the identification process. However, the scoring is ipsative, highlighting individual dynamic strengths as rated by energy, performance and use, but precluding normative comparisons with other relevant populations.

Strengthscope

The Strengthscope inventory (Brewerton and Brook, 2010) assesses individuals on a list of 24 strengths that map onto four domains of thinking, emotional, relational and execution. Like StrengthsFinder, its focus is specifically about behaviour in the workplace and provides explicit feedback on strengths related to leadership. However, there is no publicly available data on its reliability and validity, and to date the inventory has not been used in peer-reviewed publications, so it's difficult to draw conclusions about its psychometric credentials. The significant advantage of the Strengthscope inventory is that it can be used in both an individual and a multi-rater format, allowing others to rate the individual's strengths and providing data on that crucial self–other alignment.

Standout

Standout was developed by Marcus Buckingham (Buckingham, 2011) who also helped create the StrengthsFinder inventory. Standout has a different focus, using 18 talents to try to predict performance in six job families: Leader, Manager, Professional, Sales, Service and Support. The 18 talents identified are then mapped onto nine strength roles. The test then provides a variety of situations to investigate which strength roles are dominant for the individual. To test the internal reliability of the talents, Cronbach's alphas were reported from between 0.64 and 0.93. However, the only validity reported in the technical manual is content (do the items appear to measure strengths?) and face validity (do the top strength roles look right by occupation?). There is no reported data for the predictive, concurrent or incremental validity (McCashland, 2011).

Conclusion on self-report inventories for strengths

All current strength assessment measures allude to an innate ability or talent that is more fully leveraged through the identification process. This is consistent with the 'identify and use' approach where awareness of strengths alone is seen as a sufficient catalyst to instigate change. There is also clearly a degree of equivocation about what exactly strengths are with significant overlap with personality traits, competencies and virtues. In addition, the lack of normative comparisons, reliance on subjective assessment, absence of peer-reviewed publications and the utilization of opaque proprietary scoring systems make it difficult to independently assess the relative validity of these questionnaires. They also vary by the degree to which they explicitly address weaknesses rather than placing lower scoring items at the bottom of a strengths continuum. Finally, all inventories, with the exception of Strengthscope, are dependent on self-report and (as we have seen in the box on the challenges of self-report data) this can be prone to a variety of biases that promote the overestimation of scores. It is of note that, in general, the leadership inventories reviewed next have much more published data around their reliabilities and validities, partly due to their longer history of development, but partly due to greater clarity and convergence around the underlying construct to be measured. What all inventories promote is a conversation about strengths and I think it's the methodology embedded in that conversation that may be the critical factor here.

Multi-rater questionnaires

Multi-rater questionnaires or multi-source feedback (MSF) offers the opportunity to circumvent the challenges of self-assessment and gather data about the broader perception of an individual's strengths. There is a multitude of MSF inventories available, ranging from those built purely around an organization's capability framework to those that have an embedded leadership mode to those that simply ask a series of open-ended questions. Below I have identified some of the multi-raters that I think are well aligned with the strength-based approach. For a more complete review of MSF Inventories, Leslie (2013) has provided an excellent compendium.

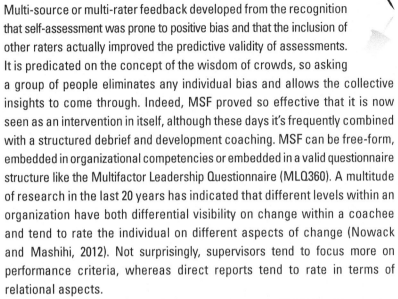

What is multi-source feedback (MSF)?

Multi-source or multi-rater feedback developed from the recognition that self-assessment was prone to positive bias and that the inclusion of other raters actually improved the predictive validity of assessments. It is predicated on the concept of the wisdom of crowds, so asking a group of people eliminates any individual bias and allows the collective insights to come through. Indeed, MSF proved so effective that it is now seen as an intervention in itself, although these days it's frequently combined with a structured debrief and development coaching. MSF can be free-form, embedded in organizational competencies or embedded in a valid questionnaire structure like the Multifactor Leadership Questionnaire (MLQ360). A multitude of research in the last 20 years has indicated that different levels within an organization have both differential visibility on change within a coachee and tend to rate the individual on different aspects of change (Nowack and Mashihi, 2012). Not surprisingly, supervisors tend to focus more on performance criteria, whereas direct reports tend to rate in terms of relational aspects.

In addition, the concept of self–other agreement (SOA) is of increasing importance. At its simplest, this is an indicator of the individual's level of self-awareness in that, if their assessment is wildly discrepant, they are usually not that aware of their impact. In addition, the direction of the discrepancy is important for understanding MSF. If the individual overrates their performance compared to others, their scores tend to come down when the feedback tool is readministered as they recalibrate their own assessment. If they underestimate their performance when compared to others, this is usually a sign of a combination of low confidence and high standards, and the coach's role is to help reduce the misalignment.

The Multifactor Leadership Questionnaire (MLQ360)

The MLQ360 (Bass and Avolio, 1997) is a 49-item questionnaire that measures nine elements of the full range leadership model (FRLM). These nine elements are divided into three categories: transformational leadership, transactional leadership, and passive/avoidant leadership. Unlike many leadership assessments, the MLQ spans the whole spectrum from highly functional and effective elements of leadership to the dysfunctional and ineffective elements. These include five elements of transformational leadership, namely:

- idealized influence attributes (eg display a sense of power and confidence);
- idealized influence behaviour (eg talk about my most important values and beliefs);
- inspirational motivation (eg articulate a compelling vision of the future);
- intellectual stimulation (eg seek different perspectives when solving problems);
- individualized consideration (eg help others to develop their strengths).

The model also includes two elements of transactional leadership, including contingent reward (eg provide others with assistance in exchange for their efforts) and management by exception active (eg keep track of all mistakes), and two elements of passive or avoidant leadership, including management by exception passive (eg fail to interfere until things become serious) and laissez-faire (eg avoid making decisions). The inventory also has three measures of leadership outcomes, including extra effort (eg heighten others' desire to succeed), effectiveness (eg lead a group that is effective) and satisfaction (eg work with others in a satisfactory way) (Bass and Avolio, 1997). It measures all items on a five-point Likert scale from 'not at all' to 'frequently if not always'.

Cronbach's alpha for the main transformational leadership factor has been reported as 0.85 (Antonakis, Avolio and Sivasubramaniam, 2003) and criterion validities vary for satisfaction (0.71), effectiveness (0.64) and performance (0.27) (Judge and Piccolo, 2004). Unlike many leadership assessments, the MLQ spans the whole spectrum from highly functional and effective elements of leadership to the dysfunctional and ineffective elements. Its strengths as an assessment tool are that it acknowledges both the strengths and weaknesses of the individual and provides them with comprehensive feedback on all nine elements of the model. There are several ways in which strengths can be extracted from the MLQ. Firstly, the relative scores on the five elements of transformational leadership indicate where strengths may lie. Secondly, the top 10 individual items are listed in the report as rated by all others. Thirdly, there is a research validated benchmark in the report that compares the coachee to a normative sample. Finally, there is a list of qualitative comments where raters identify individual strengths and development areas of the coachee.

The Leadership Versatility Index (LVI)

The Leadership Versatility Index (Kaiser, Lindberg and Craig, 2007) is predicated on the belief that performance is impacted by overdoing strengths as well as underutilizing them. This report identifies two sets of complementary domains: forceful-enabling and strategic-operational. The model asserts that to be an effective leader you have to be versatile enough to be both forceful and enabling, depending on the situation requirements, but that many individuals are lopsided, having a strong preference for one end on the continuum. The LVI embraces the strengths development model by allowing raters to rate a strength as overused, underused or about right. The coachee can then see how their strengths are impacting by level across their organization. The unique selling point of this inventory is its explicit focus on the utilization of the strength concerned with the recognition that this can be overdone as well as underdone. This approach aligns well with the link between strengths and performance discussed in Chapter 2. However, the constructs embedded in the model are fairly narrow and don't align particularly well with many of the theories of leadership discussed in Chapter 3. In terms of reliability, the inventory demonstrates sufficient inter-rater reliability (that is, above 0.7 correlation between raters). Using an independent rating of overall effectiveness as the criterion, the predictive validity of overall versatility was 0.48 (Kaiser, Lindberg and Craig, 2007).

Lominger Voices 360

The Voices 360 (Dai and De Meuse, 2007) is part of the Lominger assessment suite and rates the participant on 67 competencies as well as 19 career stallers or stoppers. The competencies come out of research by the Centre for Creative Leadership (CCL). Both the skill level and importance of the competency are rated and the rater can also indicate where a competency might be overused. The competencies sit in six factors, including strategic, operational, courage, energy and drive, organizational positioning skills, and personal and interpersonal skills. The reliability of the internal competencies is reported to lie between 0.76 and 0.93 while the test-retest reliability for factors is between 0.7 and 0.86. In terms of the criterion validity, 62/67 competencies are reported to predict performance two years later but the size of the relationship is not provided (Leslie, 2013). The strength of the Voices 360 is both the explicit attention on overdone strengths or derailers and the integration of the importance of the competency to the assessment. After all, there is little point in spending significant development time on developing or moderating a strength that is not viewed as a priority in terms of the role concerned.

Strengthscope 360

This is currently the only specific strengths-related questionnaire that is available in a 360 format. The assessment measure is described in the self-assessment section.

The Authentic Leadership Questionnaire (ALQ)

The Authentic Leadership Questionnaire (ALQ) can be administered in both a self-report and 360 format. The ALQ is divided into four subscales based on the four authentic components: relational transparency, balanced processing, self-awareness, and internalized moral perspective. Confirmatory factor analysis has supported the four dimensions of the ALQ (Walumbwa et al, 2008). Acceptable internal consistency has been consistently reported, as evident by Cronbach's alphas ranging from 0.70–0.90 (Walumbwa et al, 2008). Predictive validities for AL and organizational citizenship behaviour and organizational commitment have been reported at 0.30 and 0.28 respectively (Walumbwa et al, 2008). However, the construct of authentic leadership and its sub-domains has been challenged with the suggestion that more qualitative research is needed before converging on a measure (Cooper, Scandura and Schriesheim, 2005; Gardner *et al*, 2011).

Leadership Practices Inventory (LPI)

The LPI (Posner and Kouzes, 1993) was developed as a measure of transformational leadership that focused on the practice of leaders. The LPI is composed of five core elements, including model the way, inspire a shared vision, challenge the process, enable others to act, and encourage the heart. These dimensions show good convergent validity with other measures of transformational leadership but, unlike the MLQ, the full range of transactional and passive avoidant leadership is not assessed. The LPI is a 30-item self-report questionnaire that uses a 10-point Likert scale to rate leadership behaviours. It can be completed as both a self-assessment and in a 360-degree format. The internal reliabilities of the five elements are all reported as above Cronbach's alpha of 0.75 (Posner and Kouzes, 1993) and reported to be a valid predictor of leadership effectiveness (Tourangeau and McGilton, 2004).

Structured interview approaches

The peak experience interview

This process guides the leader through a series of semi-structured questions about when they were at their best at work, what the context was, and what specific strengths might be underpinning this heightened level of performance. This process allows flexibility and the opportunity to follow the interviewee in their strengths-related narrative. The goal here is both to elucidate examples of when the individual was at their best and also to observe them when they discuss their peak performances. Once the factors underlying their performance have been explored, it's possible to enquire about how these strengths are utilized, in what context, and how they may complement other strengths in either the individual or those around them. Consequently, rich qualitative data can be extracted in this process but it does not offer the structured framework of the self-assessment process or the other-validation of the 360 process.

The feedforward interview

A similar approach to the peak experiences interview has been outlined by Kluger and Nir (2006). Known as the feedforward interview it is a semi-structured interview derived from the principles of Appreciative Inquiry and consists of the elicitation of a key positive event, clarifying the conditions around the success of that event and crucially the clarification of future plans to implement the identified strengths. This technique functions as a strengths awareness-raising activity but provides no guidance on the type of strengths to focus on or on their titration. The approach has received some empirical support in that participants engaging in a feedforward interview process have been found to be significantly more likely to attain their goals compared to those who received a standard feedback approach (McDowall, Freeman and Marshall, 2014).

How assessment impacts methodology

There is an important but infrequently discussed connection between the type of constructs we measure and the resultant methodology applied for their development. For example, traits like those identified in the VIA are proposed for their longitudinal stability and cross-situational consistency. So, firstly, any method applied to a strength-based trait would have to acknowledge the relative immutability of the construct. Secondly, this trait is clearly located within the individual so any development methodology is most likely to be at the individual rather than dyad (two people), team or organizational level. Thirdly, such a trait-based approach does not necessarily encourage reflection around context – when is this trait most appropriately used, and how might this trait interact with other team members, contexts or environments?

Part of the art of strengths assessment is therefore matching the level that you want to intervene at with the identified strength. So a dyadic intervention would emphasize interpersonal strengths, whereas a team level intervention would emphasize complementary strengths between individuals. Practitioners need to be aware of these tendencies and reflect on both the level of desired impact and the methodological tendencies of specific strengths.

Conclusion

It is fair to say that the assessment of strengths is in its early stages of development. Consequently there is no consensus yet on the definitions of strengths, how they are best assessed or if their discriminant validity supports their separate categorization. However this does not prevent us from engaging with the methodology of a strength-based approach and drawing from insights in other areas of applied psychology. For example, there is a robust finding in selection research that a combination of personality, ability and interview is the best predictor of future candidate performance (Robertson and Smith, 2001). Consequently, I would recommend a combination of interview data on peak experiences, self-assessment on a relevant strength inventory and a multi-rater assessment to bring in the external perspective when assessing strengths. This mixed-methods approach also allows us to ascertain if the different assessment modalities align well. It's also worth recalling that the choice of what to assess strongly influences how strengths are subsequently developed. So a trait-based inventory does frequently promote an 'identify and use' approach, whereas a state-based inventory promotes more of a strengths development mindset. The real utility of the existing inventories may be that they spark a conversation around strengths and their application in the workplace. Where that conversation could go is the subject of Chapter 6.

Some questions to consider

- Consider the purpose of a strength-based assessment. How important is a reliable and valid psychometric to identify strengths?

- What are some of the challenges of self-report data?
- What are some of the benefits of MSF?
- What are some of the elements of criterion validity?
- How would you choose between different psychometrics that purport to measure strengths?

References

Antonakis, J, Avolio, B J and Sivasubramaniam, N (2003) Context and leadership: an examination of the nine-factor full-range leadership theory using the Multifactor Leadership Questionnaire, *The Leadership Quarterly*, **14** (3), pp 261–95

Atkins, P W B and Wood, R (2002) Self-versus others' ratings as predictors of assessment center ratings: validation evidence for 360-degree feedback programs, *Personnel Psychology*, **55** (4), pp 871–904

Asplund, J *et al* (2007) The Clifton StrengthsFinder® 2.0 Technical Report: development and validation, *The Gallup Organization*, Princeton, NJ

Bass, B M and Avolio, B J (1997) *Full Range Leadership Development: Manual for the multifactor leadership questionnaire*, Mind Garden Inc, Palo Alto, CA

Brewerton, P and Brook, J (2010) *Strengths for Success: Your pathway to peak performance*, Strengths Partnership Press, London

Buckingham, M (2011) *StandOut: The groundbreaking new strengths assessment from the leader of the strengths revolution*, Thomas Nelson, Nashville, TN

Carlson, J F, Geisinger, K F and Jonson, J L (eds) (2014) *The Nineteenth Mental Measurements Yearbook*, Buros Center for Testing, Lincoln, NE

Cook, M (2009) *Personnel Selection: Adding value through people*, John Wiley and Sons

Cooper, C D, Scandura, T A and Schriesheim, C A (2005) Looking forward but learning from our past: potential challenges to developing authentic leadership theory and authentic leaders, *The Leadership Quarterly*, **16** (3), pp 475–93

Dai, G and De Meuse, K P (2007) *The 2006 International VOICES® Norms: North America, Europe, Asia, and New Zealand/Australia*, Lominger International, Minneapolis, MN

Darwin, C J (1871) *The Descent of Man*, John Murray, London

Dunning, D *et al* (2003) Why people fail to recognize their own incompetence, *Current Directions in Psychological Science*, **12** (3), pp 83–87

Gardner, W L *et al* (2011) Authentic leadership: a review of the literature and research agenda, *The Leadership Quarterly*, **22** (6), pp 1120–45

Hill, J (2001) How well do we know our strengths? Paper presented at the British Psychological Society Centenary Conference, Glasgow, Scotland

Judge, T A and Piccolo, R F (2004) Transformational and transactional leadership: a meta-analytic test of their relative validity, *Journal of Applied Psychology*, **89** (5), pp 755–68

Kaiser, R B, Lindberg, J T and Craig, S B (2007) Assessing the flexibility of managers: a comparison of methods, *International Journal of Selection and Assessment*, **15** (1), pp 40–55

Kluger, A and Nir, D (2006) Feedforward first – feedback later, in Keynote address presented at the International Congress of Applied Psychology, Athens

Leslie, J B (2013) *Feedback to Managers: A guide to reviewing and selecting multirater instruments for leadership development*, Center for Creative Leadership

Linley, P A and Stoker H (2012) *Technical Manual and Statistical Properties for Realise2*, Centre of Applied Positive Psychology, Coventry

Linley, P A *et al* (2007) Character strengths in the United Kingdom: the VIA inventory of strengths, *Personality and Individual Differences*, **43** (2), pp 341–51

Macdonald, C, Bore, M and Munro, D (2008) Values in action scale and the big 5: an empirical indication of structure, *Journal of Research in Personality*, **42** (4), pp 787–799

McCashland, C R (2011) Standout: strengths assessment technical summary, downloaded from www.standout.tmbc.com

McDowall, A, Freeman, K and Marshall, S (2014) Is FeedForward the way forward? A comparison of the effects of FeedForward coaching and Feedback, *International Coaching Psychology Review*, **9** (2), p 135–46

Money, K, Hillenbrand, C and da Camara, N (2008) Putting positive psychology to work in organisations, *Journal of General Management*, **34** (3), pp 21–36

Nowack, K M and Mashihi, S (2012) Evidence-based answers to 15 questions about leveraging 360-degree feedback, *Consulting Psychology Journal: Practice and Research*, **64** (3), p 157

Peterson, C *et al* (2010) Strengths of character and work, in *The Oxford Handbook of Positive Psychology and Work*, eds P A Linley, S Harrington and N Garcea, pp 221–31, Oxford University Press, New York

Posner, B Z and Kouzes, J M (1993) Psychometric properties of the leadership practices inventory – updated, *Educational and Psychological Measurement*, **53** (1), pp 191–99

Rath, T (2007) *StrengthsFinder 2.0,* Gallup Press, New York

Rath, T and Conchie, B (2008) *Strengths Based Leadership: Great leaders, teams, and why people follow,* Gallup Press, New York

Robertson, I T and Smith, M (2001) Personnel selection, *Journal of Occupational and Organizational Psychology,* 74 (4), pp 441–72

Spain, J S, Eaton, L G and Funder, D C (2000) Perspective on personality: the relative accuracy of self versus others for the prediction of emotion and behavior, *Journal of Personality,* 68 (5), pp 837–67

Tourangeau, A E and McGilton, K (2004) Measuring leadership practices of nurses using the leadership practices inventory, *Nursing Research,* 53 (3), pp 182–89

Walumbwa, F O *et al* (2008) Authentic leadership: development and validation of a theory-based measure, *Journal of Management,* 34, pp 89–126

Evidence for the effectiveness of positive approaches to leadership development

05

CHAPTER OVERVIEW

This chapter covers:

- Levels of evidence in coaching research
- The challenges to effective research in coaching
- Evidence from generic coaching research
- Evidence from positive psychology interventions
- Evidence from positive leadership development research
- Evidence from leadership development coaching research
- Mediators and moderators in coaching research
- Strength-based coaching as a coherent methodology
- Challenges of researching coaching – lack of consensus on successful outcomes, methodological heterogeneity and protocol adherence; lack of data beyond self-report; limited use of coaching in organizations

Introduction

Evidence for the effectiveness of coaching as an effective leadership development methodology has been building steadily over the last decade (Jones, Woods and Guillaume, 2015). However, the components and methods that underpin coaching's effectiveness are still widely debated. In this chapter we will review the research on the effectiveness of some of the key components of coaching including leadership development and other positive interventions. We will also review the more sporadic literature on strength-based leadership development approaches, including my own recent study (MacKie, 2014).

Levels of evidence

Evidence for coaching in general and workplace coaching in particular is rapidly emerging. There is a variety of sources of evidence that give us confidence that coaching is an effective leadership development methodology and may offer significant advantages over other leadership development methodologies like training. Evidence has emerged from a variety of types of study that provide different degrees of confidence that the underlying methodology is responsible for any perceived changes in leadership effectiveness. At the weaker end of the continuum are the surveys that simply ask the coachee's or sponsor's opinion about coaching effectiveness. Whilst this is important from a stakeholder management perspective, it cannot preclude that the perceived effects are a function of another intervention, the placebo effect or a myriad of other potential biases and confounding variables. Next come the uncontrolled studies that look at changes over time within the same population of coachees. Depending on what variables are used as outcome measures, these studies can be very useful in recording change over time but again cannot exclude the impact of other variables beyond the coaching process. For example, there is evidence that even being on the waiting list for a leadership development intervention is sufficient to increase leadership scores, possibly due to expectancy effects and increased focus and attention on leadership style of the coachee (MacKie, 2014). Next, we have the between-subject experimental studies that compare the effects of a leadership intervention on a population against a control group of similar individuals that receive none. This allows us to be much more specific in attributing perceived change to the intervention itself as the control group partials out any non-specific effects. Finally there are the meta-analytic studies that combine selected studies to significantly increase the statistical power of the analysis (see box below).

Levels of evidence in psychological research

Not all evidence is equivalent so it is important to understand the quality of the evidentiary basis in positive organizational behaviour. Recently there have been attempts to introduce and develop the concept of evidence-based approach popular in medicine and apply it to organizational psychology (Briner and Rousseau, 2011).

Studies are usually divided along the following lines:

1 A meta-analysis. These are systematic reviews and combinations of studies that have sufficient rigour and similarity to be included in the meta-analytic analysis. The advantage of this process is statistical power – the combination of multiple studies greatly increases the number of participants under review. Smaller effects that are not visible in small sample studies can consequently be observed.

2 Randomized controlled trial (RCT). These are where the participation in the experimental or control group is randomized to avoid the bias of self-selecting participants. Participant performance during and after the coaching intervention is compared to a control group. Groups usually receive the coaching intervention after acting as a control.

3 Non-randomized controlled trial. These are where the two groups are populated on the basis of availability or organizational need rather than at random. This process can introduce more variation into the experimental and control groups which needs to be adjusted for. Also called a non-equivalent control group design.

4 Within-subjects design. This is where the population receiving the coaching is compared on some performance measure (the dependent variable) before and after coaching. The challenge for this design is that it's difficult to attribute any change to the coaching per se as you have not controlled for any other influences on the group.

5. Case studies. These are usually single case design where an individual is compared on a dependent variable before and after coaching. These type of studies often provide novel hypotheses that can then be tested in larger studies.

6. Survey data. This is simply asking the opinion of coach, coachee or sponsor regarding the efficacy of coaching. While these observations can be insightful, they are also prone to biases discussed under the challenges of self-report.

The majority of coaching research has been conducted at the level of surveys, case studies and within-subjects design. There are relatively few controlled trials of workplace coaching and even fewer that use a reliable and valid outcome measure like leadership and evaluate outcomes beyond self-report. To date we have three meta-analytic studies that have combined the most rigorous studies in coaching that demonstrate the overall effectiveness of generic coaching interventions (Theeboom, Beersma and van Vianen, 2014; Jones, Woods and Guillaume, 2015; Sonesh et al, 2015). Meta-analytic studies average the results of all the reviewed studies into a statistic known as an effect size. The most commonly utilized effect size statistic is Cohen's d. Cohen (1988) suggested that d=0.2 be considered a 'small' effect size, 0.5 represents a 'medium' effect size and 0.8 a 'large' effect size. This means that if two groups' means don't differ by 0.2 standard deviations or more, the difference is trivial, even if it is statistically significant.

Challenges to effective research in coaching

Why is the evidence for coaching in general and strength-based coaching in particular relatively limited when compared to other methodologies like training? Well, for a start, coaching as a profession is a relatively new entity and it takes time to produce a substantial evidence base. However, there are also aspects about the coaching profession in particular that make research in this area more challenging than it needs to be.

Firstly, the coaching profession has yet to converge on what a successful outcome looks like in coaching. Consequently, different studies use different outcome criteria from well-being, to goal-setting, confidence and leadership. Predictably, therefore, it's difficult to compare results across studies when the outcome criteria are not equivalent. I have argued elsewhere that leadership effectiveness should be the core outcome of workplace coaching interventions as it's a broad, relevant, reliable and easily measured construct (MacKie, 2014).

Secondly, there is the challenge of methodological heterogeneity. Studies do not follow the same methodology so it's difficult to know what the intervention consisted of, even if it is labelled as strength-based or solution-focused. Many coaching programmes simple describe themselves as eclectic with no particular method applied in pursuit of the end goal. This lack of methodological consistency is even more troubling as we have very little visibility into the coaching process itself, ie what the coach and coachee actually do in sessions. This is usually due to concerns over confidentiality. However, there are ways of investigating methodological adherence by using manuals and asking the coach or coachee about the components of the programme that circumvent these concerns over confidentiality. Coach and coachee then complete the manual after each session to indicate what components they have covered.

Thirdly, the majority of coaching research relies on self-report data and we have seen in Chapter 4 that there are concerns about the reliability of this. Why is this the case? Well it's much easier to ask one person in terms of outcomes than to ask peers, bosses and reports in a multi-rater format. Raters can drop out over time and this can be an issue in terms of reliable measurement. However, the goal of coaching in organizations is usually to impact more positively on others so other raters do seem essential in understanding how far a change in coachee behaviour ripples through the organization (O'Connor and Cavanagh, 2013).

Finally, it is relatively rare to find organizations that agree to participate in coaching research. It can be time consuming for participants to fill in the requisite forms, and organizational need often mitigates against a truly randomized process. There is also the concern of managing the political fallout if the study fails to show any significant outcomes or a poor return on investment (ROI).

Evidence for the effectiveness of positive approaches

Evidence from generic coaching research

Individualized coaching has become an increasingly popular method for facilitating and supporting leadership development processes

(Carey, Philippon and Cummings, 2011). Coaching has historically been asserted to be primarily a skills or insight acquisition process that is content neutral and can be applied to a wide range of development goals in a range of contexts (Whitmore, 2010). Consequently, multiple theories, models and processes can be inserted into the coaching framework (Grant, Green, and Rynsaardt, 2010). However, recently the content neutral stance has been challenged with the emergence of specialist models of coaching (Elliott, 2005).

In a comprehensive review of coaching effectiveness, Grant *et al* (2010) found a total of 156 outcome studies that examined the effectiveness of coaching in all areas including the workplace. Of these 101 were case studies, 39 were within-subject designs and only 16 were between-subject designs (ie utilized a control group). This wasn't a meta-analytic study so no overall effect size was computed for these studies but, if we apply our research criteria discussed above, the number of studies that were conducted in the workplace, using leadership as a dependent variable, and measured outcomes beyond self-report, shrinks alarmingly. However, these reviews of studies do suggest some of the necessary components of effective coaching.

There is increasing evidence that effective executive coaching requires a core set of common principles at its foundation (McKenna and Davis, 2009; Grant *et al*, 2010). These include a collaborative working alliance between coach and coachee, the integration of activities to raise self-awareness of the coachee, some clearly defined goals and specific actions to achieve them. Many of these common principles, designed to raise self-awareness and set and attain relevant goals, are well aligned with the core constructs of positive psychology. Despite this alignment, there remains an ongoing debate about both the relative contributions these core components make to a successful outcome in coaching and the degree to which differing theories and techniques influence successful coaching interventions (de Haan and Duckworth, 2013; MacKie, 2007). Research in the profession has yet to evolve to the point when clearly delineated theoretical approaches to coaching, including strength-based approaches, are compared in a reliable and valid manner.

There are now three meta-analytic studies on the effectiveness of coaching that have sought to combine the most rigorous studies into a systematic review of coaching outcomes. Theeboom, Beersma and van Vianen (2014) found 18 studies of sufficient rigour to be included in their analysis. Of those only four were conducted in the workplace, used a between-subject methodology and collected data other than self-report. The average effect size for these four studies was 0.08 to 0.36 which would be considered small to medium-sized effects. A more recent meta-analysis (Jones, Woods and Guillaume, 2015) examined 17 studies conducted in the workplace. They also addressed the criterion specification problem by focusing on outcomes relevant to organizations like skill acquisition and individual results. Their analysis found effect sizes of coaching and outcome criteria ranging from 0.28 to 1.24 with individual level results achieving the biggest impact. However, there was no distinction made between self and other sourced feedback so the broader impact of the coaching studies is not known.

In conclusion, there is growing evidence for coaching's effectiveness as a methodology for developing skills, abilities and awareness in the workplace. Specifically goal attainment, well-being, stress reduction, and self-efficacy all do seem to improve after coaching when measured by the coachee themselves. What is less clear is how others view change and how change extends beyond the impact on individual variables to organizational performance criteria like leadership. Equally it is not apparent from this data whether all coaching methodologies are equivalent in achieving these outcomes.

Evidence from positive psychology interventions

Evidence for coaching effectiveness comes in both direct and indirect forms. There is converging evidence for the effectiveness of strength-based approaches in other domains. Positive psychology with its emphasis on building on strengths and enhancing confidence and positive emotion is increasingly being applied in an executive coaching context (Biswas-Diener and Dean, 2007). There is growing evidence of the effectiveness of positive psychology interventions in clinical populations (Seligman *et al*, 2005) but to date, the majority of the organizational research has focused on the enhancement of well-being criteria, such as mental health and engagement rather than performance criteria like the development of transformational leadership behaviours (Linley, Harrington and Garcea, 2010; Wood *et al*, 2011). Focusing on a strength-based approach to leadership coaching provides the opportunity to test the performance impact of a specific element of the positive psychology paradigm.

Drawing on the work in positive psychotherapy, there is evidence for the benefits of increased positive mood states and emotions that are predicted to emerge from a strength-based approach (Peterson and Seligman, 2004). Similarly, Harter, Schmidt and Hayes (2002) found individuals who regularly use their strengths report more engagement in their work. Furthermore, there is some evidence that when managers emphasized performance strengths in their direct reports, their performance increased significantly. The converse was also reported, that focusing on weaknesses reduced performance (Corporate Leadership Council, 2002). In addition to potentially enhancing employee performance, engagement and retention, there is also increasing evidence for the impact of a strength-based approach on the subjective well-being of the individual. Increased psychological well-being (Govindji and Linley, 2007), reduced stress (Wood *et al*, 2011) and increased goal attainment (Linley *et al*, 2010) have all been correlated with a strength-based approach to coaching. Despite this range of positive outcomes, there remains little consensus on how best to leverage strengths. Much of the practitioner focus consequently appears to be that of a commitment to a strengths identification process rather than the adherence to a specific strength development methodology or protocol (Lopez and Snyder, 2009). This has made the identification of specific strength-based mediators and moderators problematic.

A number of studies have supported the use of a range of techniques derived from positive psychology both to develop positive emotional states and more optimistic perspectives in a coaching context (Arakawa and Greenberg, 2007; Fredrickson, 2001). Positive psychology has supported the use of self-concordant goals in coaching with evidence to suggest that this alignment with personal values enhances goal attainment (Burke and Linley, 2007). Furthermore, positive psychology has championed the utlilization and enhancement of strengths in the coaching process amidst claims that this provides greater engagement and developmental gains for the individual and the organization (Govindji and Linley, 2007; Linley, Willars, and Biswas-Diener, 2010). However, strengths coaching can both be viewed as an approach or method of coaching where strengths are identified and developed in the pursuit of other goals and an outcome of coaching where the coachee gains a clearer understanding of their strengths and how to leverage them as a result of the coaching process (Carter and Page, 2009).

In conclusion there is analogous evidence from positive psychological interventions that emotional states, concordant goals and employee engagement can all be enhanced through the application of strengths in a coaching context. Our next challenge is to investigate the impact of such interventions on organizationally relevant outcomes like leadership and other performance criteria.

Evidence from positive leadership development

There is compelling evidence that leadership can be developed over time via a variety of methods and processes including coaching (Day, 2001; Day, Harrison and Halpin, 2012). There have been several meta-analyses that have examined the combined effectiveness of leadership development interventions. Collins and Holton (2004) examined 83 formal leadership training studies that looked at enhancing leadership performance at the individual, team and organizational levels. Of these, 19 studies used a longitudinal controlled design to assess objective outcomes at the level of increased leadership expertise and found an overall effect size of 1.01. However, the range of effect sizes was from -0.28 to 1.66 suggesting the presence of as yet unidentified design and delivery elements of the programme that make a significant difference to the effective development of leadership.

Avolio *et al* (2009) performed a meta-analysis of 200 laboratory and field studies of leadership development. They found an overall small effect size of leadership change after the development intervention of 0.65 (versus 0.35 for control groups) and could find no significant difference depending on the theory utilized in the intervention. Despite this relatively small combined effect size, the standard deviation of outcomes was 0.80, suggesting significant variation in the effectiveness of the studies assessed. Overall they concluded that despite the heterogeneous mix of theory, dependent variables, developmental processes and outcomes, leadership could be enhanced over a short period of time using a variety of methodologies.

These meta-analyses provide convincing evidence that leadership ratings can change significantly over time but tell us little about the impact of those changes on subsequent performance criteria. Fortunately, the performance impacts and outcomes of some of the more recent models of leadership, especially transformational leadership, have been extensively studied. Wang *et al* (2011) performed a meta-analysis of 113 studies investigating the impacts of transformational leadership on task (eg in-role performance), contextual (eg organizational citizenship behaviour) and creative (eg innovation) performance outcomes. They reported a mean correlation between individual level performance and transformational leadership of 0.25 using non-self-report measures.

In conclusion, there is considerable evidence that leadership is more state-like in its ability to be enhanced by specific development interventions like coaching and that improved leadership impacts directly on objective performance criteria. The specific methodologies that may lead to more significant changes in leadership, together with the processes that result in changes in leadership, remain equivocal. Strength-based approaches offer the opportunity to empirically test a specific strengths assessment and development methodology to ascertain its impact on developing leadership effectiveness.

Evidence from leadership development coaching

Coaching has been used in a leadership development context in a number of ways including building and transferring skills, raising self-awareness and enhancing motivation (Hernez-Broome and Boyce, 2011; Passmore, 2015). However, as the coaching profession matures, there is an increasing emphasis on defining effective methodologies and applying them to organizationally relevant performance criteria like leadership effectiveness. This is where a strength-based methodology offers real hope for enhancing leadership development effectiveness in organizations.

There are several reasons as to why leadership coaching poten-tially may offer the most effective pathway to integrate positive states and traits into the development of effective leaders. Firstly, the coaching process is individually tailored to the needs of the coachee rather than part of a more generic leadership training process, making it a more specific, relevant and concordant experience. Secondly, coaching shares the affirmative bias of positive psychology with its focus on goal attainment and individual professional development (Burke and Linley, 2007). Thirdly, coaching routinely includes the tripartite pro-cess of assessment, challenge and support, offering the capacity to identify and develop specific positive constructs like strengths (Ting and Riddle, 2006). Finally, coaching is an iterative process that facili-tates the transfer of learning by its quotidian setting and reviewing of specific actions (Carey, Philippon and Cummings, 2011). Consequently, it has been claimed that positive psychology coaching provides the potential vehicle for the integration of the insights and concepts of positive psychology into the leadership development process (Biswas-Diener and Dean, 2007; Kauffman, 2006).

Leadership coaching also offers a potential solution to the problem of comparing different outcomes across coaching studies. The concept of comparative efficacy is further impeded by the lack of consensus on what constitutes a successful outcome in executive coaching, which in turn is a function of the breadth and complexity of issues that can be addressed under the umbrella of coaching in organizations (Feldman and Lankau, 2005; Lee, 2003). This diversity of outcomes has in some way been ameliorated by the emergence of domain specific coaching that seeks to impact on a particular element of individual performance. Thus, leadership coaching has been explicit in its focus on raising the leadership capacity of the coachee in the organizational context (Elliott, 2011). This focus is contrasted with executive coaching, which defines the level of the coachee but gives no indication of the focus of the coaching process. Given this current methodological heterogeneity, a strength-based coaching methodology offers the opportunity to test the efficacy of a specific and coherent approach to the development of leadership skills and behaviours. While there is growing evidence of the effectiveness of positive psychology interven-tions, the majority of the organizational research has focused on well-being criteria like mental health and engagement rather than performance criteria such as the development of transformational leadership behaviours (Linley, Harrington and Garcea, 2010).

Cilliers (2011) reported one of the few studies to actively take a positive psychological approach to leadership coaching. He defined positive psychology leadership coaching as a focus on the people aspects of learning, growth and change in order to positively impact on the intrapersonal and interpersonal aspects of leadership. The study examined the impacts of positive leadership coaching on 11 leaders in a financial organization. Participants engaged in 10 experiential coaching sessions that focused on work engagement, coherence, values, resourcefulness and locus of control. Using discourse analysis in a series of single case designs, Cilliers identified six emergent themes. These included engagement in the role, role complexity, emotional self-awareness, self-authorization (where the locus of perceived control resides internally rather than waiting for others to provide direction) and facilitating the growth of others. Whilst this study presents some important qualitative associations between positive psychology and leadership coaching, no quantitative data was reported and no post-intervention outcomes evaluated so the broader impact of this intervention is difficult to ascertain. Nonetheless, this developing research base suggests positive psychology has both a coherent theoretical framework and a growing empirical validation that could provide a firm foundation for executive and leadership coaching (Seligman, 2007). Focusing on a strength-based approach to leadership coaching provides the opportunity to test the performance impact of a specific element of the positive psychology framework.

In my own research on strength-based leadership coaching (MacKie, 2014) I specifically set out to investigate the impacts of a strength-based methodology on leadership criterion as measured by both the participant and others within their organization. We used a between-subject non-randomized control group design with 37 leaders and managers from an international NFP organization. In keeping with Chapter 4, we used a combination of interview, self-report and multi-rater data to assess strengths in the coachee. The outcome variable was the MLQ360 that measures transformational leadership as well as the less desirable elements of the full-range leadership model. Crucially we administered this in a 360 format so we looked at the impact of the strength-based coaching on others in the organization before and after the intervention.

The study used a strength-based coaching protocol specifically developed for this research study. At its core was the concept of strengths development (see Chapter 6) where coachees were encouraged to take a growth-orientated approach to thinking about their strengths. Each coachee picked a realized strength to moderate, an unrealized strength to develop, and a weakness to manage. Participants experienced six sessions of coaching over a three-month period and then swapped roles, the control group becoming the participants and vice versa. In this study each coachee received the Realise2 inventory, the MLQ360 and a strength-based interview. The rater consistency over time was checked and made no difference to the analysis. In analysis of the results, I combined all the five elements of transformational leadership into a composite score to see how transformational leadership as a whole varied over time after the strength-based coaching. The results were unequivocal. The coaching cohort achieved a highly significant effect size three times that of the control group over the same period. This effect was significant for all other raters but not for the participants themselves. This is a critical finding as the majority of coaching research uses only self-report data and if we had done so on this occasion we would not have found significant effects.

So why didn't the participants themselves report significant changes in their leadership behaviours? One of the factors involved here is self–other alignment in rating scores. When participants are given their MLQ360 feedback, if they find they have rated themselves higher on transformational leadership than all others, they tend to compensate for this when the test is readministered after the coaching. It's one of the common ways to correct for the biases in self-assessment and, in this case, that effect was more powerful for the coachee than the effects of the coaching. However, all others, and especially those higher up in the organization, did see significant change and it's the other group we are trying to positively impact on after coaching.

In addition to the significant changes in transformational leadership after strength-based leadership coaching, we also found positive changes in leadership outcomes. Leadership outcomes are what raters report in terms of extra effort, effectiveness and satisfaction of the coachee's leadership style before and after coaching. So after coaching the raters of the coachee were willing to provide additional discretionary effort to the coachee as a function of positive changes in their leadership style. This is another critical finding as leadership is ultimately trying to unlock additional resources from peers and direct reports. So what was it about the strength-based coaching that proved so effective? To test this we rated adherence to the coaching manual from both the coach and the coachee perspective to test how much of the strength-based protocol they adhered to and how influential this was in achieving the positive changes in transformational leadership. Again, we found that both manual and coach adherence to the strength-based protocol was predictive of positive changes in transformational leadership, indicating that it was the strength-based components of the programme that were influential in achieving positive leadership change in the coachees.

Mediators and moderators in coaching research

Moderators effect the direction and strength of independent variable (eg type of coaching) and dependent variable (eg leadership outcomes). Possible moderators included developmental readiness, personality variables, sessional alliance and coach credibility. In my research, I made the pragmatic decision to focus on coachee variables that, in my own practitioner experience, seemed to have the potential to predict important variations in the response to coaching. These included positive states around change readiness and positive traits from the core self-evaluation literature.

Mediators are the mechanism by which the independent variable (eg type of coaching) is able to directly influence the dependent variable (eg leadership capacity). Potential psychological mediators can include mastery, self-efficacy and self-insights. In my own study, I considered the strength-based approach to be a major mediator of enhanced leadership effectiveness but also recognized that the mediator–moderator distinction can become blurred when variables can potentially act as both. Testing this required the calculation of both manual and protocol adherence which is why the manualization process was essential. (See Figure 5.1 for a diagrammatic representation of the mediator–moderator distinction.)

FIGURE 5.1 Potential mediators and moderators in leadership coaching effectiveness

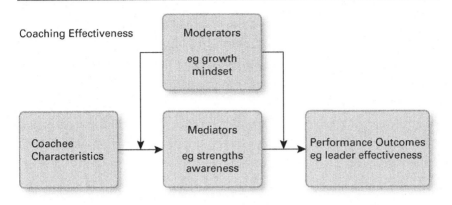

Strength-based leadership coaching as a coherent methodology

The issue of methodological coherence also needs to be addressed to control some of the multiplicity of variables that can occur under a typical coaching methodology. The evidence outlined earlier in this chapter suggests there is a developing evidence base for coaching in general and leadership coaching in particular. However, there remains an ongoing debate about both the relative contributions which core components make to a successful outcome in coaching and the degree to which differing theory and techniques influence successful coaching interventions (MacKie, 2007; de Haan and Duckworth, 2013). The strength-based approach for developing leaders offers both a coherent theoretical framework, empirical validation and a well-developed range of psychometric assessment tools that could bring some methodological consistency to the delivery of executive coaching (Kauffman, 2006).

A strength-based methodology, however, requires more than just the identification and leverages of strengths in the coachee. Part of the challenge of advocating a strength-based approach is to define exactly what that entails. Strengths can be identified through a variety of standardized inventories like the Realise2 (Linley and Stoker, 2012). How those strengths are subsequently developed requires some consistency in order that a similar process is applied across different coaching engagements. Manualization provides a potential solution to the challenge of methodological inconsistency and provides an objective index of adherence to the protocol. Manualization also offers the opportunity to be specific and consistent about what is meant by strengths development (Biswas-Diener, Kashdan and Minhas, 2011). Developing strengths involves the process of optimal titration (Linley *et al*, 2010), managing the potential overuse of strengths (Kaiser and Kaplan, 2009), pairing strengths with other similar competencies (Zenger, Folkman and Edinger, 2010) and aligning strengths with the broader business goals and with intrinsic interests (Govindji and Linley, 2007; Linley *et al*, 2010). These elements of strengths development are more fully discussed in Chapter 6.

Conclusion

The evidence base for strength-based coaching as an effective leadership development methodology is developing rapidly. Part of the support for this approach comes from the foundationary evidence of both the leadership development and the positive psychology literature. In addition, evidence is growing for the specific effectiveness of strength-based approaches to leadership coaching. The coaching profession has advanced to the point where three meta-analytic studies have now confirmed the effectiveness of coaching in general but have not yet confirmed the specific elements of the coaching methodology responsible for mediating change including strengths. My own research programme is providing convincing evidence for the positive roles of strengths in achieving significant changes in leadership capacity. Research also needs to move beyond the over-reliance on self-report data and agree on specific outcome criteria to aid cross-study comparisons.

Some questions to consider

- Why is conducting coaching research in organizations so challenging?
- What are the limitations of relying on self-report data in coaching research?

- Why are RCTs so rare in coaching research, and do we need them?
- Can the research in strength-based coaching develop independently of reliable and valid strength-based psychometrics?
- What coaching outcomes are relevant to your organization?

References

Arakawa, D and Greenberg, M (2007) Optimistic managers and their influence on productivity and employee engagement in a technology organization: implications for coaching psychologists, *International Coaching Psychology Review*, 2 (1), pp 78–89

Avolio, B J *et al* (2009) A meta-analytic review of leadership impact research: experimental and quasi-experimental studies, *The Leadership Quarterly*, 20 (5), pp 764–84

Biswas-Diener, R and Dean B (2007) *Positive Psychology Coaching: Putting the science of happiness to work for your clients*, Wiley, Hoboken, NJ

Biswas-Diener, R, Kashdan, T B and Minhas, G (2011) A dynamic approach to psychological strength development and intervention, *Journal of Positive Psychology*, 6 (2), pp 106–18

Briner, R B and Rousseau, D M (2011) Evidence-based I–O psychology: not there yet, *Industrial and Organizational Psychology*, 4 (1), pp 3–22

Burke, D and Linley, P A (2007) Enhancing goal self-concordance through coaching, *International Coaching Psychology Review*, 2 (1), pp 62–69

Carey, W, Philippon, D J and Cummings, G G (2011) Coaching models for leadership development: an integrative review, *Journal of Leadership Studies*, 5 (1), pp 51–69

Carter, D and Page, N (2009) Strengths coaching, in *The Encyclopedia of Positive Psychology*, ed S J Lopez, pp 949–57, Blackwell, Oxford

Cilliers, F (2011) Positive psychology leadership coaching experiences in a financial organization, *SA Journal of Industrial Psychology*, 37 (1), pp 1–14

Cohen, J (1988) *Statistical Power Analysis for the Behavioral Sciences*, Lawrence Erlbaum Associates, Hillsdale, NJ

Collins, D B and Holton, E F (2004) The effectiveness of managerial leadership development programs: a meta-analysis of studies from 1982 to 2001, *Human Resource Development Quarterly*, 15 (2), pp 217–48

Corporate Leadership Council (2002) *Performance Management Survey*, Washington, DC

Day, D V (2001) Leadership development: a review in context, *The Leadership Quarterly*, 11 (4), pp 581–613

Day, D V, Harrison, M M and Halpin, S M (2012) *An Integrative Approach to Leader Development: Connecting adult development, identity, and expertise*, Routledge, New York

de Haan, E and Duckworth, A (2013) Signalling a new trend in executive coaching outcome research, *International Coaching Psychology Review*, 8 (1), pp 6–19

Elliott, R (2005) The parameters of specialist professional leadership coaching, in *Evidence-Based Coaching: Contributions from the behavioral sciences*, eds M Cavanagh, A M Grant, and T Kemp, pp 111–26, Australian Academic Press, Bowen Hills, QLD

Elliott, R (2011) Utilising evidence-based leadership theories in coaching for leadership development: towards a comprehensive integrating conceptual framework, *International Coaching Psychology Review*, 6 (1), pp 46–70

Feldman, D C and Lankau, M J (2005) Executive coaching: a review and agenda for future research, *Journal of Management*, 31 (6), pp 829–48

Fredrickson, B L (2001) The role of positive emotions in positive psychology: the broaden-and-build theory of positive emotions, *The American Psychologist*, 56 (3), pp 218–26

Govindji, R and Linley P A (2007) Strengths use, concordance and well-being: Implications for strengths coaching and coaching psychologists, *International Coaching Psychology Review*, 2 (2), pp 143–53

Grant, A M, Green, S L and Rynsaardt, J (2010) Developmental coaching for high school teachers: executive coaching goes to school, *Consulting Psychology Journal: Practice and research*, 62 (3), pp 151–68

Grant, A M *et al* (2010) The state of play in coaching today: a comprehensive review of the field, *International Review of Industrial and Organizational Psychology*, 25 (1), pp 125–67

Harter, J K, Schmidt, F L and Hayes, T L (2002) Business-unit-level relationship between employee satisfaction, employee engagement, and business outcomes: a meta-analysis, *Journal of Applied Psychology*, 87 (2), pp 268–79

Hernez-Broome, G and Boyce, L A (eds) (2011) *Advancing Executive Coaching: Setting the course for successful leadership coaching*, Jossey-Bass, San Francisco, CA

Jones, R J, Woods, S A and Guillaume, Y R (2015) The effectiveness of workplace coaching: a meta-analysis of learning and performance outcomes from coaching, *Journal of Occupational and Organizational Psychology*

Kaiser, R B and Kaplan, R E (2009) When strengths run amok, in *The Perils of Accentuating the Positive*, ed R B Kaiser, pp 57–76, Hogan Press, Tulsa, OK

Kauffman, C (2006) Positive psychology: the science at the heart of coaching, in *Evidence Based Coaching Handbook: Putting best practices to work for your clients*, eds D R Stober and A M Grant, pp 219–53, Wiley, Hoboken, NJ

Lee, G (2003) *Leadership coaching: From personal insight to organisational performance*, CIPD Publishing, London.

Linley, P A, Harrington, S and Garcea, N (2010a) *Oxford Handbook of Positive Psychology and Work*, Oxford University Press, New York

Linley, P A, Willars, J and Biswas-Diener, R (2010) *The Strengths Book*, CAPP Press, Coventry

Linley, P A *et al* (2010b) Using signature strengths in pursuit of goals: effects on goal progress, need satisfaction, and well-being, and implications for coaching psychologists, *International Coaching Psychology Review*, 5 (1), pp 6–15

Linley, P A and Stoker H (2012) *Technical Manual and Statistical Properties for Realise2*, Centre of Applied Positive Psychology, Coventry

Lopez, S J and Snyder, C R (2009) *Oxford Handbook of Positive Psychology*, Oxford University Press, New York

MacKie, D (2007) Evaluating the effectiveness of executive coaching: Where are we now and where do we need to be?, *Australian Psychologist*, 42 (1), pp 310–18

MacKie, D (2014) The effectiveness of strength-based executive coaching in enhancing full range leadership development: a controlled study, *Consulting Psychology Journal: Practice and Research*, 66 (2), pp 118–37

McKenna, D and Davis, S L (2009) Hidden in plain sight: the active ingredients of executive coaching, *Industrial and Organizational Psychology*, 2 (3), pp 244–60

O'Connor, S and Cavanagh, M (2013) The coaching ripple effect: The effects of developmental coaching on well-being across organisational networks, *Psychology of Well-Being*, 3 (1), pp 1–23

Passmore, J (ed) (2015) *Leadership Coaching: Working with leaders to develop elite performance*, 2nd edn, Kogan Page, London

Peterson, C and Seligman, M E (2004) *Character Strengths and Virtues: A handbook and classification*, Oxford University Press, New York

Seligman, M E P (2007) Coaching and positive psychology, *Australian Psychologist*, 42 (4), pp 266–67

Seligman, M E P *et al* (2005) Positive psychology progress: empirical validation of interventions, *American Psychologist*, 60 (5), pp 410–21

Sonesh, S C *et al* (2015) The power of coaching: a meta-analytic investigation, *Coaching: An International Journal of Theory, Research and Practice*, 8 (2), pp 73–95

Theeboom, T, Beersma, B and van Vianen, A E (2014) Does coaching work? A meta-analysis on the effects of coaching on individual level outcomes in an organizational context, *The Journal of Positive Psychology*, 9 (1), pp 1–18

Ting, S and Riddle, D (2006) A framework for leadership development coaching, in *The Center for Creative Leadership Handbook of Coaching*, eds S Ting and P Scisco, pp 34–62, John Wiley and Sons, San Francisco, CA

Wang, G *et al* (2011) Transformational leadership and performance across criteria and levels: a meta-analytic review of 25 years of research, *Group and Organization Management*, **36** (2), pp 223–70

Whitmore, J (2010) *Coaching for Performance: GROWing human potential and purpose: the principles and practice of coaching and leadership*, Nicholas Brealey Publishing, London

Wood, A M *et al* (2011) Using personal and psychological strengths leads to increases in well-being over time: a longitudinal study and the development of the strengths use questionnaire, *Personality and Individual Differences*, **50** (1), pp 15–19

Zenger, J H, Folkman, J R and Edinger, S K (2011) Making yourself indispensable, *Harvard Business Review*, **89** (10), pp 84–92

Strengths development

06

CHAPTER OVERVIEW

This chapter covers:

- Strengths development planning
- Developing professional expertise
- Positive goal selection
- Goals gone wild?
- Goal prioritization
- Strengths overdone, underdone, misused, weaknesses
- Managing weaknesses and derailers
- Strengths pairing, alignment, utilization and awareness
- Developing specific leadership strengths
- The context of development – who, what, where, when, how?

Introduction

Once we have assessed strengths with the variety of formats discussed in Chapter 4, there are a number of tasks required to turn these insights into actions. Firstly, we need to identify which of the fully utilized strengths, underutilized strengths and weaknesses we need to attend to in order to enhance leadership capability. This is a process primarily of prioritization and alignment with the goals of the business in which the individual coachee works. Secondly, we need to be clear what developmental methodologies are appropriate for the strength concerned. For example, if a strength is being fully utilized, then a key development process is learning how to recognize and manage overuse. However, if a strength is underutilized, then pairing it with a complementary strength is an effective way to increase its utilization. If a weakness has been identified then it is key to identify the magnitude of its impact. A fatal flaw requires a very different focus from a low level of a capacity that is not relevant for the individual's job role.

Once strengths have been prioritized they are usually placed into a development plan. Development planning is the crucial activity that takes these insights from the assessment phase and acts as a bridge to the strength development phase. There are a number of components in development planning (see box below) but it usually involves a process of defining the vision for success, leveraging related strengths and, crucially, outlining specific actions that will lead to the development of the identified area. In my own experience as a leadership development practitioner, I find repeatedly that the quality of the plan is significantly correlated with the size and sustainability of the change that the individual makes in terms of enhancing their leadership capability.

What is strengths development planning?

Strength development planning provides a structure to take the insights apparent in the strengths identification phase through to the actions required to develop new skills and behaviours. Development planning should be linked to your career planning so it helps to map out your ambitions one, three and five years out so that you can check alignment with the development goals you have set yourself.

Development planning has five key components:

1 What is the theme you wish to develop? Is this an over-, under- or fully utilized strength? These should relate to a leadership or competency area, eg coaching and developing your direct reports.

2 How will you define and measure success? How will you know when you are there and what is the vision? Try and describe this in detail at a behavioural level. How do these criteria align with the business objectives?

3 What complementary strengths can you leverage in the pursuit of this goal? Are there any supporting behaviours around this strength that can be leveraged?

4 What actions will you take? These need to be SMART (Specific, Measureable, Attainable, Realistic and Timely). Specificity is key here – what will you do, with whom, and when? What would you like to experiment with and get feedback on?

5 Finally, how will you monitor and maintain your progress? Who will hold you accountable and support your development? Broadly speaking, the more people that know about your goals, the more accountable you are.

Developing professional expertise

Strength-based leadership development can be viewed as a form of the development of professional expertise. This work has been pioneered by Anders Ericsson (2009) over the last 30 years. He defines expertise as very much a skill development process that follows a sequence from cognitive development where skill acquisition is deliberate, conscious and slow to an associative stage focused on enhancing speed to an automatic phase where the skill is no longer conscious. There are interesting parallels between Ericsson's work and the strengths development literature in that both have as their definitions the need for a superior reproducible performance. The expert performance approach, as it is known, tries to identify the difference between elite and average performers – what is it that elite leaders, managers of athletes do differently from those that are considered average? The evidence clearly suggests there is much more to expertise than experience. In fact there is some suggestion that newly qualified professionals can be more effective than their seasoned counterparts precisely because they have not automated their skills and are still consciously reflecting on them.

During studies of multiple domains of expertise including music, medicine and leadership, some consistent themes have emerged (see box below on characteristics of expertise). At its core these themes include a resistance to automaticity through the development of ever more complex representations. For example, in leadership, instead of acquiring one model of leadership, mastering its components and gradually letting these insights become automatic, an expert would be continually acquiring new models of leadership, looking at the parallels and differences and pulling out inferences, common themes and points of difference. In other words, they would remain actively and consciously engaged with the material. The second core element of the development of expertise is the concept of deliberate practice. Typically this requires 10 years or 10,000 hours of deliberate, goal-orientated and mastery-focused practice (Ericsson, Prietula and Cokely, 2007).

Characteristics of expertise (Ericsson and Moxley, 2012)

- Experts seem to acquire a large number of complex algorithms to evaluate future scenarios.

- Experts 'chunk' data to simplify more complex scenarios.

- Experts engage in meta-cognitive reflection that reduces the urge to automaticity.

- Experts put the effort in – around 10,000 hours of deliberate practice at a minimum.

- Expertise is highly domain specific and does not seem to generalize well.

- Experts have a talent for practice, persistence and skill mastery.

It is worth reflecting on the implications of the characteristics of professional expertise for the development of strength-based leadership capacity. Given that expertise appears to be highly domain specific, leaders really need to know their sector, organization and context. This is especially important when considering lateral hires for other sectors or industries. Expert leaders also require motivation, drive, influence and resilience. Expertise alone is not enough to be an effective leader. Finally, developing leadership expertise requires the support, engagement and mentoring of others. It does not occur in a vacuum but rather as a synergistic interaction between the individual, the supportive organization culture and the growth mindset of the leader's sponsors (McCall, 2010).

Positive goal selection

Goal setting is one of the most established techniques to enhance performance. Numerous studies testify to the positive effects of setting specific, measureable and concordant goals that are mastery-orientated (Locke and Latham, 2002; Lyubomirsky, Sheldon and Schkade, 2005). There is a general consensus that successful goals need to be:

- intrinsic in nature rather than prescribed by others;
- self-concordant or congruent with personal values;
- positive and success-orientated rather than avoiding issues;
- mastery-orientated rather than aimed at an arbitrary performance criterion;
- aligned with business strategy and outcomes;
- achievable in the relevant time horizon.

However, this consensus has been recently challenged (see box below).

Goals gone wild?

A contentious review of the research has challenged the orthodoxy around the universal benefits of goal setting. Ordóñez *et al* (2009) have questioned the merits of this approach suggesting that goal-setting can:

- narrow attention when they are too specific;
- be confusing when there are multiple and potentially competing goals;
- can be too challenging and therefore inspire risk-taking or helplessness;

- inhibit learning when performance goals are applied in complex environments;

- inhibit intrinsic motivation if goals are externally proscribed.

In a response to these criticisms, Locke and Latham (2009) concur with many of the concerns although not with the scholarship around them. Goal setting, like any behavioural technique, comes with the caveat that it takes significant expertise to make the complex look simple.

Goal prioritization

Once you have assessed your strengths, how do you then select which ones to focus on in terms of development? There are a number of ways to do this. Firstly, as this is a book about leadership strengths, you can draw inspiration from what the researchers in the field have identified as crucial strengths required for effective leadership. Despite there being multiple models on this topic (see Chapter 2 for a review of these domains) there remain significant areas of overlap and communality amongst the various strength models. For example, there is typically a domain for managing self (including areas of emotional management and integrity), a domain for managing others (including building relationships and influencing others), a domain for managing change (including thinking strategically and stakeholder management), and a domain for getting results (including innovating, goal setting and developing others).

Secondly, you can map your strengths onto the goals and priorities of the business to check where the alignment is. This can be done by mapping strengths onto organizational competencies specific to the business concerned or onto the relevant elements of the strategic plan. The final element of prioritization is to pick goals that are challenging yet attainable in the time parameters you are working within.

Generic strengths development

Once you have selected the goals and priorities, it's time to consider how to develop the strengths concerned. In introducing this topic to leaders there are several metaphors that can facilitate understanding and shifting the mindset from a categorical to a more dimensional mode. The key element here is to encourage the notion of amplitude, so the concept of a dial that can either turn up or down the expression of a strength can be very useful. Equally, a rating scale that includes negative numbers in its range helps reinforce the concept that strengths can be underutilized as well as overutilized. Strengths development can be functionally divided into four distinct categories, namely strengths awareness, alignment with the business goals, effective pairing with other strengths both within the individual and across the team and finally strength utilization. Building in a dimensional rating scale to your development planning will facilitate this (see Figure 6.1).

FIGURE 6.1 Thinking dimensionally about your strengths

Strength Awareness	Strength Alignment	Strength Pairing	Strength Utilization
High	High	High	High/Too Much
↑ Applying strengths with situational and systemic awareness	↑ Strengths fully aligned and integrated with team/business goals	↑ Fully leveraging complementary behaviours to strengths	↑ Significant overuse of this strength
Consciously applying my strengths	Most strengths aligned with team/business goals	Linking some strengths to complementary behaviours	Too much application on occasions
Thinking about how to engage my strengths	Strengths somewhat aligned with team/business goals	Beginning to identify complementary behaviours	Could still apply a bit more
Performance without reference to strengths	Strengths independent of team/business goals	Working on individual strengths in isolation	Not applying my strengths enough
↓ Low	↓ Low	↓ Low	↓ Low/ Too little
Current Rating (1–10)	Current Rating (1–10)	Current Rating (1–10)	Current Rating (–5 to +5)
Desired Rating (1–10)	Desired Rating (1–10)	Desired Rating (1–10)	Desired Rating (–5 to +5)

How to develop fully utilized strengths

Fully utilized strengths are known by the individual and are already being applied successfully across a number of situations. The goal of developing a fully utilized strength is one of optimal titration, maintaining their strength in the zone of peak performance. Recall in Chapter 2 we considered how strengths are related to performance with the most likely scenario being an inverted U distribution. The goal here is to keep performance at the top of the inverted U without heading down the other side towards overuse. The risk here is derailment due to an over-application of the strength concerned. Two approaches will assist the leader here in calibrating their strengths to maximum effectiveness. Firstly, they need to think dimensionally about their strengths. Strengths lie on a continuum from under- to overuse so it's important to begin the conversation on what overuse would look like. When does confidence become arrogance and strategic thinking become operational disengagement? Secondly, the leader needs to recall the generic relationship between strengths and performance. There is only a small band of the curve that is optimal, so what are the markers either side that will indicate a departure from the zone of optimal performance?

This example brings us to a second key strategy of managing fully utilized strengths – the concept of complementary pairing. The goal of developing a strength that is fully utilized is one of diversification rather than excessive utilization. This concept has been pioneered by Zenger, Folkman and Edinger (2011) who have mapped out the complementary behaviours of 16 key leadership capabilities. It's based on the idea that each strength is supported by a number of behaviours that may not be as fully developed as the strength itself. Continuing the example above of the technical expert who can overplay the detail focus, one of the complementary strengths of technical expertise is communicating powerfully and broadly. So a strength in detail and analysis is complemented by the additional capacity to communicate these insights at the right level for the right audience with the right amount of supporting documentation.

How to manage overutilized strengths

Overused strengths are often a product of the uncritical adoption of the 'identify and use' approach to strengths development. The idea that more of a strength is necessarily a good thing can become deeply embedded and it's important to challenge these assumptions about strengths utilization during the development process. Another moderating factor in the overuse of strengths is the lack of flexibility or versatility. This pattern can become apparent with the repeated application of the same strength to a variety of circumstances, eg the solution to ambiguity is always to over-prepare on familiar topics, or the solution to challenging employees is always to be directive and dominant. This type of inflexibility is commonly connected to career derailment. So techniques that again introduce dimensionality into the leader's thinking will be effective here in breaking down the categorical models into more subtle dimensions so that they internalize the thinking 'when do I apply this strength, at what amplitude, and how will I know if I have over-leveraged?'

A common strength I see over-leveraged particularly in technical experts, is that of focusing on the detail. PowerPoint presentations contain a mass of data, explanations include the granular detail, and conversations tend to be at the operational level. In the right context, this is a strength to bring rigour and empiricism to the discussion. However, with more senior audiences, this frequently leads to frustration as they rarely want to step through the detail (although they do want to know it's there if needed). The adverse impact of such an over-leveraged strength is that the question can be asked about the individual's strategic capability. Can they see the themes and patterns in the data and, if so, why are they not articulating them?

Another useful concept in managing overuse is the idea of moderating strengths with complementary strengths, especially those that promote self-control (Niemiec, 2014). This concept comes from the arena of character strengths where specific strengths like humility which help regulate excess have been identified. This is a very useful conversation to promote with leaders as, not only does it promote the concept of strength moderation, but it also introduces the idea that strengths can be associated with the regulation rather than just the expression of behaviours.

How to develop underutilized strengths

Underutilized strengths present a different challenge to the risk of overuse. The first question is why an individual may be underutilizing their strengths. Assuming they are aware of their strengths, the next question would be: are they motivated to apply them? My own experience operating in an Australian context for the last 10 years tells me there are cultural influences at play here. Many executives I work with are either embarrassed to reflect too heavily on their strengths or impeded by a reluctance to self-promote. To counteract this mindset, one option is to stress the benefit to the organization of having individuals fully leverage their strengths. Individuals may also underestimate their strengths (similar to poor self–other alignment in a 360-degree feedback process). The reasons for this again can be complex but include low levels of confidence, perfectionism and self-criticism or the consequence of a strong development orientation (Sosik, 2004). Development options here may include assessing readiness for change (more fully discussed in Chapter 7) and addressing the reasons behind low levels of confidence or the tendency towards perfectionism.

Once the motivational factors have been addressed, the level of competence in the strength to be developed needs to be evaluated. Strengths, like skills, are developed through deliberate practice and can be ranked from baseline to mastery. The same model discussed earlier under the development of professional expertise can be applied here. For example, individuals may have an unrealized strength in confidence or self-efficacy that can be enhanced by acquiring the skill of making internal, stable and specific attributions after achieving success in a particular area. This is a case of skill and strength development through the acquisition of a specific technique derived from attributional theory. Complementary pairing can also be used in the development of an underutilized strength. A common example in managers and even executives is an underutilized strength in building relationships and rapport, resulting in an avoidance of challenging conversations and holding others accountable. This strength can be developed by the recognition of the 'both–and' implicit in this situation. It is possible to be both agreeable and have challenging conversations with others. One sets up the foundation for the other.

Once the skill issue has been addressed, the extent of the application of the strength can be evaluated. This approach again draws on the skill acquisition literature that suggests the way to consolidate and maintain a skill is through continuous application in multiple and varied scenarios. This is where standard coaching techniques like the GROW model (Alexander, 2006) can be usefully applied through the generation of multiple options for consolidation (see box on page 109).

The GROW model in coaching

The GROW model (Alexander, 2006) is one of the foundational constructs in coaching and has been consistently applied since its development more than 20 years ago. The acronym stands for:

Goal – *what is the goal or purpose of the coaching programme? This can include the peak experiences activity described in Chapter 4 to facilitate the vision of a future where strengths are more fully and functionally applied.*

Reality – *where is the individual now in terms of the desired end point? This is a form of self-assessment that can be augmented by a variety of other-assessment and feedback measures.*

Options – *what possible actions can you generate that will move you from where you are to where you want to be? What strengths can you identify, leverage, titrate, complement and regulate?*

Wrap up or will – *what will you commit to doing in terms of the actions generated under options. Where are the opportunities to apply strengths and who will provide feedback on their amplitude and effectiveness?*

The GROW model has been developed and modified over time and one of the more interesting variations is the Intentional Change Model (ICM, Boyatzis, 2006). The ICM model incorporates a couple of elements from positive leadership development including the concept of the ideal self (similar to the peak performance technique in Chapter 4) and the notion of developing both strengths and gaps in relation to the attainment of the ideal self.

How to manage weaknesses including career derailers

One of the key challenges in dealing with weaknesses is to differentiate those which are marginal and can be made irrelevant from those that have the elements of a fatal flaw imbedded in them and must be addressed (Zenger *et al*, 2012). Kaiser (2009) has emphasized the importance of both context and amplitude in terms of strength development. All strengths have the potential to become derailers if overplayed (Kaiser, 2009) and this focuses attention on not just raising awareness of strengths as in the 'identify and use' approach, but also considering how they are applied, in what context and with what intensity. The leadership derailment literature confirms the risks of encouraging the unregulated amplification of strengths. There is no quick and easy way to delineate between the two, as much of this assessment is context-dependent and role-specific. However, there are repeating themes that appear in the derailment literature that suggest fatal flaws often coalesce around the following themes (MacKie, 2008):

- failure to delegate;
- failure to build a team;
- aloofness and arrogance;
- insensitivity to others;
- over-reliance on a single sponsor;
- inability to change or adapt to transitions.

The other method to ascertain the impact of the weakness is to engage the talent management system in which the organization is incumbent. Most line managers and talent specialists are fairly candid about behaviours that will stall careers and potentially derail leaders. As an external consultant, it's important to understand which behaviours are culturally anathema and which are just antagonistic to effective leadership. It is important also to factor in career stage at this point as behaviours that some organizations positively promote at early stages in the leader's career (eg excessive work hours) can become liabilities at later stages. So, firstly, to distinguish a fatal flaw from a weakness, the centrality of the weakness to the current and potential future roles needs to be considered. Secondly, how differentiated is the weakness? For example, how many other competencies does it impact? Thirdly, consider how severe the weakness is – is the leader at baseline on a skill that they should have mastered at their career stage? There is no reason why fatal flaws cannot be addressed with the same techniques outlined above with the caveat that chronic trait-like deficits will take longer to turn around. However, it's important to remember that addressing fatal flaws is necessary but not sufficient in terms of building exceptional leadership performance. The elimination of the negative is a separate process from the cultivation of the positive but, crucially, a critical impediment to leadership development has been removed.

How to manage misused strengths

Misused strengths are those that are developed in the pursuit of self-serving and potentially unethical pursuits. Positive leadership is by definition, the pursuit of a task or goal that is usually self-transcendent and certainly does no harm to the broader organization or community. Misused strengths are usually a function of leveraging those not aligned with other-orientated values or a failure to consider the moral and ethical consequences of their development.

TABLE 6.1 Strengths and their development strategies

Strength	Technique
Underutilized	Complementary pairing
	Awareness raising
	Peak experiences
Overutilized	Apply moderating strengths
	Optimal titration
	Derailment management
Fully Utilized	Goal alignment
	Application onto weaknesses
	Contextual diversification
Misused	Values clarification
	Apply moderating strengths

Developing specific leadership strengths

There is currently a state of healthy tension in the field of leadership development between those who emphasize that being exceptional in a few areas is the pathway to enhanced leadership performance (eg Folkman and Steel, 2012) and those who are more cautious about the positive impact of strength enhancement (eg Kaplan and Kaiser, 2013). Hopefully by now it is apparent that these views are not mutually exclusive and the focus may just be on a different area of the same dimension. For those who promote the notion of excelling in a few areas, one of the best developed models is that of the development of specific complementary leadership skills through the process of cross-training (Zenger, Folkman and Edinger, 2011). As described in Chapter 2, Zenger *et al* (2012) have developed their own leadership model with 5 domains and 16 competencies within those domains. However, their own research has led them to conclude that these leadership strengths can be successfully enhanced by the development of complementary strengths closely aligned to the competency concerned. So, for example, developing a strategic perspective can be enhanced by improvements in innovation, communication and business acumen. Developing others, however, is enhanced by developing competency companions in the areas of developing effective feedback processes, inspiring and motivating others and practising self-development. These competency companions have the effect of diversifying the original leadership strength and encouraging its development through the concurrent development of multiple supporting leadership behaviours.

Authentic leadership development

Authentic leadership contains four key elements: balanced processing in decision-making, an internalized moral perspective, relational transparency with others, and self-awareness (Walumbwa *et al*, 2008). Research into the construct validity of authentic leadership suggests that these four scales appear to form part of a higher order factor of authenticity that is distinguishable from the concept of transformational leadership. Authentic leadership development (ALD) involves directly targeting these four sub-themes as potential development areas. Self-awareness can be raised by a myriad of techniques and psychometrics and is something in common with virtually all leadership development processes. Relational transparency can be achieved by being open with followers about your leadership development process and inviting feedback on perceived changes. ALD is also closely aligned to psychological capital (PsyCap). Optimism, for example, is one of the core elements of PsyCap and can be learned through attribution training (Seligman, 2011). PsyCap can also be developed in followers as a result of being led in a more transformational way (Luthans *et al*, 2007).

Full Range Leadership Development

Full Range Leadership Development (FRLD) aims at specifically enhancing the transformational elements of the full range leadership model (Sosik and Jung, 2011). For example, idealized influence which is about building trust with followers and acting with integrity can be directly developed by encouraging the coachee to disclose their most important values and beliefs or how ethical considerations are embedded in their decision-making. Inspiring others is grounded in positive emotions which themselves can be developed through PsyCap interventions or connecting goals to purpose and values. Inspiring others is mediated by regulating your own levels of self-confidence and ensuring your presentations are engaging and impactful. These are strengths that can be further leveraged by identifying complementary strengths around this theme. Intellectual stimulation is about encouraging innovation through being curious, open to alternatives, avoiding the tendency to converge too quickly on solutions and, crucially, allowing others to come up with novel solutions. Finally, individualized consideration is about coaching and developing others. This is essentially effectively coaching direct reports through a combination of understanding their individual drivers and aspirations, helping them to develop their strengths and promoting an environment of developmental readiness. Providing effective feedback is a strength that can be leveraged in the pursuit of developing others more effectively. The quickest way to discover your strengths as a transformational leader is to take the MLQ360. This then gives you an excellent platform from which to develop your transformational leadership strengths.

Summary and conclusion

This chapter is about effectively developing your strengths after the process of identification. Developing leadership strengths is similar to developing any professional competency and there are lessons to be learned from the acquisition of expertise and the importance of effective goal setting in the pursuit of enhanced leadership effectiveness.

Strengths development can either be a generic process where individual strengths are aligned around specific leadership goals or a more specific focus on the underlying elements of positive leadership theories. Either way, thinking dimensionally about strengths and managing their utilization through alignment, pairing and leveraging complementary strengths is an effective way to accelerate your strength-based leadership development.

Some questions to consider

- How can you think more dimensionally about strengths?
- What type of leadership strengths lend themselves most to development?
- In what situation can weaknesses not be ignored?
- Have you considered developing a strength to moderate other strengths?
- When would you develop specific versus generic leadership strengths?

References

Alexander, G (2006) Behavioural coaching – the GROW model, in *Excellence in Coaching: The industry guide*, ed J Passmore, pp 83–93, Kogan Page, London

Boyatzis, R E (2006) An overview of intentional change from a complexity perspective, *Journal of Management Development*, **25** (7), pp 607–23

Ericsson, K A (2009) *Development of Professional Expertise: Toward measurement of expert performance and design of optimal learning environments*, Cambridge University Press, New York

Ericsson, K A, Prietula, M J and Cokely, E T (2007) The making of an expert, *Harvard Business Review*, **85** (7/8), pp 114–21

Ericsson, K A and Moxley, J H (2012) The expert performance approach and deliberate practice: implications for studying creative performance in organizations, in *Handbook of Organizational Creativity*, ed M Mumford, pp 141–67, Academic Press, New York

Kaiser, R B (ed) (2009) *The Perils of Accentuating the Positive*, Hogan Press, Tulsa, OK

Kaplan, R E and Kaiser, R B (2013) *Fear Your Strengths: What you are best at could be your biggest problem*, Berrett-Koehler, Oakland, CA

Locke, E A and Latham, G P (2002) Building a practically useful theory of goal setting and task motivation: a 35-year odyssey, *American Psychologist*, **57** (9), pp 705–17

Locke, E A and Latham, G P (2009) Has goal setting gone wild, or have its attackers abandoned good scholarship?, *The Academy of Management Perspectives*, **23** (1), pp 17–23

Luthans, F *et al* (2007) Positive psychological capital: measurement and relationship with performance and satisfaction, *Personnel Psychology*, **60** (3), pp 541–72

Lyubomirsky, S, Sheldon, K M and Schkade, D (2005) Pursuing happiness: the architecture of sustainable change, *Review of General Psychology*, **9** (2), pp 111–31

MacKie, D (2008) Leadership derailment and psychological harm, *InPsych: The Bulletin of the Australian Psychological Society*, **30** (2), pp 12–13

McCall, M W (2010) Recasting leadership development, *Industrial and Organizational Psychology*, **3** (1), pp 3–19

Niemiec, R M (2014) *Mindfulness and Character Strengths: A practical guide to flourishing*, Hogrefe Verlag, Göttingen

Ordóñez, L D *et al* (2009) Goals gone wild: the systematic side effects of overprescribing goal setting, *The Academy of Management Perspectives*, **23** (1), pp 6–16

Seligman, M E P (2011) *Learned Optimism: How to change your mind and your life*, Vintage, New York

Sosik, J J (2004) *The Dream Weavers: Strategy-focused leadership in technology-driven organizations*, IAP, Charlotte, NC

Sosik, J J and Jung, D D (2011) *Full Range Leadership Development: Pathways for people, profit and planet*, Taylor and Francis, New York

Walumbwa, F O *et al* (2008) Authentic leadership: development and validation of a theory-based measure, *Journal of Management*, **34**, pp 89–126

Zenger, J H, Folkman, J R and Edinger, S K (2011) Making yourself indispensable, *Harvard Business Review*, **89** (10), pp 84–92

Zenger, J H, Folkman, J R, Sherwin, R H and Steel, B A (2012) *How to Be Exceptional: Drive leadership success by magnifying your strengths*, McGraw-Hill, New York

Coaching for positive leadership development in organizations

07

CHAPTER OVERVIEW

This chapter covers:

- Readiness for individual and organizational change
- Identifying the stakeholders
- Picking a positive leadership model, eg MLQ360
- Assessing strengths through MSF
- Ensuring uniformity of delivery
- Socializing the model and aligning to strengths
- Goals – setting positive goals with business relevance
- Evaluation – measuring success using formative and summative outcomes

Key components of coaching for PLD in organizations

This chapter is about putting what we have already learned about assessing and developing strengths in a leadership context into practice. The process begins with determining the readiness of both the individual and the organization for a strength-based approach to leadership development. Despite the inherent appeal of the approach, not all organizations will be engaged by such a methodology. There are numerous factors that may mediate readiness, but some key ones include how a strength-based approach aligns with current (implicit and explicit) models of leadership already extant in the organization. What are the assumptions around a strength-based approach? Are these largely positive, negative or neutral?

Readiness to change and develop

Readiness for change and development is something that should be assessed prior to the beginning of any leadership development process. The reason for this is simply to do with managing the limited resources organizations have at their disposal for people development and ensuring the organization gets a sufficient return on their development investment. It is a popular myth that everyone is ready for and can benefit from leadership coaching. A myth that is regularly debunked by the variable effect sizes in coaching and leadership outcome studies, by the between-participant variance seen within the evidence base and by the everyday experience of those involved in the leadership development business who experience the range of engagement, responses and outcomes to fairly uniform leadership development processes. At the organizational level, too, support for the leadership development initiative is vital if changes are to be successfully transferred into the workplace. Key variables here again include how the participants will be supported in terms of time to consolidate developmental insights, what opportunities will be provided to consolidate learnings and how the programme will be integrated into the existing learning and development framework. The two concepts of change and developmental readiness have been proposed to articulate this construct more fully.

The concept of developmental readiness has been put forward as a potential predictor of effective outcomes in leadership development (Avolio and Hannah, 2008; Hannah and Avolio, 2010). This combination of motivation and ability to change is potentially seen as a prerequisite for effective engagement in the leadership development process. Developmental readiness is a more focused element of the broader construct of change readiness (Franklin, 2005). This broad construct brings together a number of underlying concepts, including beliefs about the possibility of change, willingness to experience discomfort in the pursuit of change, and awareness of potential areas of focus.

Developmental readiness has been defined as 'both the ability and the motivation to focus on, make meaning of and develop new and more complex ways of thinking that position you to more effectively assume leadership roles' (Avolio, 2010). The concept was partially derived from the literature on stages of change (Prochaska and DiClemente, 1982) which suggested that, in any change process, individuals go through the stages of precontemplation (unaware of the need for change), contemplation (thinking about change), preparation (getting ready to make the change) and action (actually doing the requisite behaviours). Clearly suggesting leadership development to someone who is in the precontemplation stage is unlikely to be met with engagement or enthusiasm. In addition, the sheer variability of responses to leadership coaching, even when as many of the coach and organizational variables are held as constant as possible, does suggest that the coachee is bringing their own behaviours, qualities and mindsets that are having a significant impact on coaching outcomes. Developmental readiness is seen as a potential prerequisite of successful leader development, in that it attempts to identify and assess key individual criteria for the change inherent in positive leader development to occur.

Assessing individual and organizational readiness

At this stage in the development of the concept of readiness for change and development, assessing individual readiness for change is a matter of practitioner skill and experience rather than the reliance on the administration of a reliable and valid psychometric. Some typical questions include:

Individual readiness questions

- Are you prepared to experience discomfort in the pursuit of enhanced leadership effectiveness?

- What's your motivation for engaging in this leadership development process (LDP)?

- How will this process change the way you think of yourself as a leader?

- What resources do you have to sustain and support your development?

- What type of goals have you set yourself in terms of engaging with this LDP?

- How will you encourage others to give you the necessary developmental feedback?

Organizational readiness questions

- How aligned is the strength-based approach with existing leadership development philosophies?

- What is the prevailing mindset around leadership development? Is it growth or fixed?

- Is the executive leadership team a sponsor? Are they participating?

- How will the process be supported internally?

- Are there any other competing change initiatives under way at this time?

- How will this process be integrated into the Learning and Development framework?

Mapping the stakeholders

It has been argued that for coaching to be effective, we need coach, coachee and organizational factors to be in alignment (see Figure 7.1 on page 127). This usually means there are a minimum of three key stakeholders in the coaching process:

- *The coachee*: Key factors include how committed are they to the process, are they ready, do they have the resources, what's their history of self-development, do they take responsibility for their development?

- *The line manager*: Key factors include how transparent have they been with the coachee, is their leadership style compatible with a coaching approach, how sensitive are they to change, how supportive are they of the coachee, what's the quality of the relationship with the coachee?

- *The HR sponsor*: Key factors include where is the coachee in the talent pool, what is the talent philosophy of the organization, are the line manager and HR sponsor aligned, where are the boundaries of confidentiality, how does coaching connect to other talent development opportunities?

At the start of any coaching engagement it's important to map the stakeholders in the process. This is especially true if the coaching has a remedial element to it.

Selecting a strength-based leadership model

Once readiness to engage in leadership development has been assessed, it's time to pick a conceptual model that will support the assimilation of the strength-based approach. Ideally the model is closely linked to the assessment process chosen to identify strengths (discussed in Chapters 3 and 4). Factors impacting on this selection include reliability and validity, compatibility with existing leadership models, the seniority of the coachees and the model's sensitivity to change. Ideally this is a model that will lend itself to a repeat assessment at the end of the intervention to evaluate outcomes and ROI.

Identifying strengths in the individual through MSF

In assessing strengths, it is advisable to utilize both a self-report measure and a multi-rater to ensure there are no blind spots in the diagnostic process. Whilst multi-rater instruments are generally very effective at circumventing the biases of self-report, the range and objectivity of raters is another important consideration. It is generally effective here to combine both individual preferences in rater selection and include mandatory criteria like all direct reports to ensure the coverage is broad and representative. This ensures high quality feedback that will enhance the strengths awareness process.

Feedback is a key component of coaching in organizations. Its purpose is multifactorial, to raise awareness, to identify strengths and weaknesses, to calibrate self–other ratings, to understand different ratings by levels in organizations and to gain insight into the developmental readiness of both the individual and the organization. The most commonly utilized feedback is multi-source feedback (MSF), otherwise known as 360-degree feedback. MSF is increasingly popular in organizations and routinely used in leadership coaching interventions. Its ubiquity suggests that it is worth spending some time on both how to interpret and maximize the utility of MSF data.

MSF data depends on a number of assumptions that have been subject to intensive scrutiny in the research literature. Firstly there is an assumption that other-ratings are valid predictors of performance and carry in them some additional information that is not available to the coachee. There is significant evidence for this, in that numerous studies have shown that individuals tend to overrate themselves, known as leniency bias (Atkins and Wood, 2002). Of even greater concern is that there is evidence to suggest that those who are objectively rated as performing poorly on a task show the greatest tendency to overrate themselves (Dunning *et al*, 2003). These findings have led to intensive interest in the area of self–other alignment and what it means for interpreting MSF data. Interestingly, there do appear to be some areas that are more accurately assessed by the individual, although these are normally characteristics with low observability, eg anxiety or self-esteem. In considering feedback on strengths, it is worth considering how observable this might be to others and how easy it might be to evaluate. Intrapersonal strengths by definition are more private, whereas interpersonal strengths should display a significant degree of public manifestation.

Socializing the coachee to the strength-based model

Organizations and the leaders within them will come with a variety of prejudices as to the meaning of a strength-based approach to leadership development. Areas to cover in your initial discussions with both the organization and the coachee include:

- A strength-based approach does not deny the presence or relevance of weaknesses.
- There is significant evidence for the link between strength-based approaches and enhanced leadership effectiveness.
- Strengths can be both leveraged directly and applied to addressing weaknesses.
- The type of strengths you develop matters. You will get more benefit from enhancing states and skills than you will addressing traits.
- There are multiple benefits to strength-based approaches beyond enhanced leadership effectiveness, including engagement, positivity, well-being and goal attainment.
- A strength-based approach is much more engaging for the coachee and therefore facilitates readiness and participation.

Ensuring the coachee is ready for each session

What does the coachee need to do in terms of preparation to maximize the gains from each session? Ideally, they will reflect, review and act. Reflection on the previous session is achieved through considering questions like:

- What strengths did you identify?
- What strengths do you overuse?
- What strengths do you underuse?
- What strengths work well together?
- What situations bring out the best in you?
- What actions can you take to further leverage your strengths?

Focusing on where changes are made allows the coachee to review progress and monitor change. What are they noticing in terms of:

- The strengths they've identified?
- How they are applying those strengths?
- How they are utilizing their strengths – not over- or underplaying?
- The type of goals they are setting themselves?

Finally, they need to have acted on the insights from the previous session. So if they have identified an overused strength, what have they done to alert themselves when this is happening? If it is an underutilized strength, where else have they found to apply this strength and what was the outcome? Ideally the coachee should come to the session with this preparation. When I am meeting my own mentor, I prepare an e-mail of topic areas beforehand and send it through to give them a chance to prepare.

Ensuring the process supports the content

There is a long-standing debate in other areas of applied psychology (eg psychotherapy) about the relative contributions of technique and process in terms of delivering sustainable change (MacKie, 2007). The technique in this case is the strength-based approach to leadership coaching and the process is how this coaching is delivered, that is, what non-specific qualities the coach brings to the process (eg challenge and curiosity). Perhaps because of the psychological origins of many coaching techniques, a number of assumptions including the importance of common factors, like the coaching relationship, have been adopted somewhat uncritically into a coaching format. Consequently, it has taken a while for concepts like accountability and challenge to embed themselves in coaching models. A notable exception to this is the FACTS model (Blakey and Day, 2012).

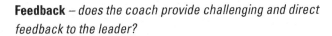

The FACTS model of coaching

FACTS is an acronym for:

Feedback – *does the coach provide challenging and direct feedback to the leader?*

Accountability – *does the coach hold the leader accountable for actions they commit to?*

Challenge – *does the coach challenge the leader in a constructive way and encourage them to experience the discomfort that change involves?*

Tension – *how does the coach hold in tension in the process to ensure key issues are fully explored without damaging the underlying relationship?*

Systemic thinking – *how does the coach remain focused on both the situational factors impacting the leader and the leader's response to these factors?*

The FACTS model itself evolved out of the financial crisis that created a demand for coaching focused on organizational need rather than individual preference. The FACTS model implicitly challenges the mindset of more traditional coaching approaches that can be generalized as high support and low challenge. Applying this to strength-based leadership coaching, we can have a positive methodology augmented by a more challenging delivery process to ensure optimum outcomes. Concurrently, the FACTS process guards against one of the criticisms of strength-based approaches, that is, focusing only on the positive and avoiding difficult conversations (see Chapter 10 for a further elaboration of this issue).

Ensuring uniformity of delivery – coach variables

When applying a strength-based leadership coaching intervention across the top tier of an organization, how do you ensure a reasonable degree of uniformity in the delivery of the leadership coaching process? This is a significant issue as, due to concerns over confidentiality and a reluctance by the coaching profession to endorse specific factors related to superior outcomes in leadership coaching, there is relatively little transparency in individual coaching engagements. Consequently, it is not uncommon for participants to have a significantly different experience, despite being part of the same coaching process. There are a number of ways to bring a degree of uniformity to what can be a very heterogeneous process. Firstly, coaching training in the chosen methodology is essential prior to beginning the intervention. This will ensure that at least the core concepts are universally applied and with a degree of systemization. Training can include the more conceptual areas, like models and frameworks, to the more operational, like number of sessions, types of goals, development planning and organizational objectives. The leadership coaching process can also be manualized (MacKie, 2014) to really encourage adherence to the strength-based protocol. Manualization involves writing down the key components for each coaching session for both coach and coachee to encourage adherence to the protocol. The challenge here is to maintain openness and receptivity to the emergent needs of the coachee, whilst utilizing the manual to provide structure and rigour to the process. The possible coach, coachee and organizational variables that can affect strength-based leadership coaching are summarized in Figure 7.1.

Ensuring strategic goal alignment

The effectiveness of the leadership coaching will, of course, be enhanced if there is good alignment between the business and individual goals and objectives. This is one of the key criteria for goal

FIGURE 7.1 Technique and process factors in strength-based leadership coaching

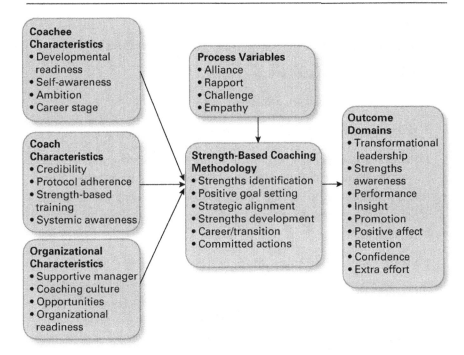

selection (see Chapter 6) and also an important topic for the coach briefing prior to the beginning of the programme. This can be supported by the encouragement of goal selection around self, team and organization, or through embedded linkages in the development plan that connects organizational competencies or objectives to the individual development goals. Table 7.1 shows a sample goal selection process. In this example, 'develops others' is the obvious choice for strengths development.

Goal selection from the MLQ360

Once you have discussed your strengths from the MLQ360, you need to converge on some goals for the coaching. Normally 2–3 are ideal for this duration of coaching.

Consider the following questions:

1. What I am energized/enthusiastic about changing?

2. Which goals are aligned with the organizational imperatives?

3. Which goals are aligned with my values?

4. Which goals are mastery-orientated?

5. Which goals will help me manage better the challenges I face?

Table 7.1 shows an example of the transformational leadership strengths of an individual leader derived from the MLQ360. In this case, developing others is the strength to develop further, as it combines a high skill level, an intrinsic interest in developing this strength, and is aligned with the organizational need.

TABLE 7.1   Strength development options from MLQ360

Strength/ Competency	High Skill	Passion/ Energizing	Organizational Need	Total
Builds trust	x			1
Acts with integrity				
Inspires others				
Encourages innovation				
Develops others	x	x	x	3

Ensuring visibility of change

The visibility of change is a critical matter in leadership coaching, especially for those whose self–other alignment is poor. There is significant evidence that change is perceived differentially within an organization (MacKie, 2015b) and these changes are to some degree mediated by the self-awareness of the coachee. Individuals who overrate themselves compared to other raters can be at risk of derailing (ie suffering a significant setback in their career) and may be less receptive to feedback, but the gap between self and others can also act as a motivator to change. Individuals who underrate themselves when compared to others are often self-critical and perfectionistic and can be sceptical of the evidence that others perceive them to be more effective than they see themselves (Nowack and Mashihi, 2012). Overraters tend to self-correct over time and this effect can mask gains made in leadership coaching. Consequently, the ratings of others in terms of change can be highly validating.

There is also some evidence to suggest that raters at different levels focus on different aspects of the leader, with supervisor ratings being more closely correlated with external performance criteria, whilst direct reports (those reporting directly into the participant) focus on more interpersonal and relational criteria (Nowack, 2009). In reviewing repeat MSF surveys it is important to incorporate this tendency into the analysis. It is also important to mediate a discussion between the coachee and their line manager as to how changes in leadership behaviour will be observed. Sharing the coachee's development plan is an excellent medium through which to facilitate this discussion.

Ensuring the sustainability of change

There is concerning evidence (Baldwin and Ford, 1988) that much of the learning that occurs in a training environment is not effectively transferred to the workplace, and the learnings that are transferred can be rapidly eroded over time. The support provided for those coachees who have been through a leadership coaching process largely depends on the degree of coaching sophistication of those around them. Line managers and peers who have undergone a high level of coach training themselves are best placed to provide support for coachees following a programme. This is where individual coaching can link effectively with previous programmes, especially those that include a Manager or Leader as Coach element. At the very least, the line manager of the coachee needs an awareness of the coaching process, the goals established and the outcomes achieved. This is best achieved through the ongoing involvement of the line manager throughout the coaching process – known as three-cornered coaching (Standards Australia, 2011). This typically involves a three-way discussion with coach, coachee and line manager at the beginning of the coaching programme to clarify goals, periodic alignment sessions between coachee and manager throughout the coaching process, and a further three-way discussion to review achievements and consider next steps at the end of the programme.

The coaching goals can then be integrated into the organizational development plan and periodically reviewed as part of the existing performance review process. There is no doubt that the broader the disclosure of the coaching goals, the greater the probability of maintaining focus and gains on them.

Ensuring reliable and valid outcomes and ROI

Connected to the above issue of training transfer and sustainability is the issue of ensuring that reliable and valid outcomes and a healthy return on investment (ROI) are achieved from a strength-based leadership coaching process. While the potential domains on evaluation after leadership coaching are vast, the psychometrics used in the strengths identification phase are the obvious measures to repeat after the end of the coaching programme. I would argue that these measures, by necessity, have to include multi-rater feedback around a well validated leadership measure like the MLQ360. However, these instruments give data on leadership changes, which may be attributable to coaching but not on subsequent performance improvement in the coachee's team and the organizational metrics on which their performance is judged. Finally, the timing of any evaluation needs to be considered. Reactions to coaching can be assessed almost immediately, but what will this tell you about skill acquisition of performance improvement? Other changes in terms of increased leadership capability, leading to enhanced follower engagement, leading to additional discretionary effort in followers, leading ultimately to enhanced job performance (however measured) will inevitably take time to work their way through an organization.

The evaluation of training interventions in organizations, including leadership, has traditionally been dominated by the Kirkpatrick model that suggested change could be monitored and evaluated at four discrete stages or levels (Kirkpatrick, 1959, 1977). Level 1 captured the reaction of the participant to the leadership programme and usually involved ratings of client satisfaction. Level 2 involved assessing what the coachee learned from the coaching programme. This attempted to measure changes in specific knowledge, skills or attitudes that could be attributed to the coaching programme. Level 3 focused on behavioural change, including leadership behaviour. Finally, Level 4 related the results of the coaching programme to the attainment of organizational objectives. The summative models of evaluation have evolved since Kirkpatrick first suggested his criteria and additional levels looking specifically at ROI have been added (Hamblin, 1974). The benefits of the Kirkpatrick model are that it offers a framework for the evaluation to occur within and emphasizes that subjective self-assessment alone is insufficient for effective evaluation. Kirkpatrick's four-stage process is viewed as a 'taxonomy of outcomes' rather than a scientific model of evaluation (Holton, 1996).

Subsequently, two types of evaluation have emerged in the leadership evaluation literature: summative evaluation, which looks at the completed outcomes of the leadership intervention, and formative evaluation, which consists of process-orientated questions that focus on programme improvement (Ely *et al*, 2010). This is a useful distinction as it ensures that the method of delivery is evaluated alongside the traditional Kirkpatrick taxonomy. Ely *et al* (2010) suggest the summative evaluation framework can incorporate much of the Kirkpatrick taxonomy with Level 1 being expanded to include the client's perception of the coach's competence and their satisfaction with the client–coach relationship. Level 2 is expanded to include self-awareness as well as increased behavioural flexibility. Level 3 remains focused on leadership behaviours and is ideally incorporated into a pre- and post-coaching 360-degree feedback process. Finally, Level 4 remains focused on results but includes the impact on peers, direct reports, and other stakeholders, as well as the total return on investment (ROI).

In addition to the traditional summative process, Ely *et al* (2010) stress the need for a formative evaluation to improve the quality of the training intervention. This focuses on process rather than outcome criteria and helps to identify any implementation barriers to attaining the leadership coaching objectives. They include coachee expectations, the competence of the coach, the quality of the client–coach relationship and the coaching process itself. It also provides the coachee the opportunity to provide feedback on the elements of the process and method they found most effective. The coaching method can be divided into specific and non-specific factors depending on the preferences of the coachee and the theoretical orientation of the coach. Specific factors might include elements of strength-based coaching, whilst non-specific factors includes elements like empathy and rapport. Client variables can include both organizational and coachee factors given that the organization provides the context in which the coaching will occur (see Figure 7.1).

Another interesting debate that has influenced the evaluation of training and coaching research is that of common versus specific factors previously mentioned (McKenna and Davis, 2009). The common factors position asserts that there are common processes at play across coaching engagements and that these can form the basis of effective evaluation. Common factors are seen as mainly occurring in the coaching relationship and involve qualities like expectancy, empathy, rapport and positive regard. These are hypothesized to be significantly more influential than any specific technique and therefore tend to minimize the significance of specialist training in the coach (MacKie, 2007). The specific factors position reverses the relative importance, placing the specific coaching technique as the key orchestrator of change and the relationship factors as necessary but not sufficient for sustained behavioural change. My position on this is that the specific factors are crucial in leadership coaching, while common factors provide the platform for delivery. My own research (MacKie, 2014) demonstrated that protocol adherence was predictive of positive leadership change suggesting that the specific factor, in this case strength-based leadership coaching, was critical in enhancing transformational leadership.

Conducting a leadership coaching evaluation

Formative evaluation questions

Formative evaluation looks to examine the process of coaching and ascertain what worked in terms of its delivery and what could be improved for the next iteration (MacKie, 2015a). Areas that are typically examined include:

Coaching process

Did the coach...

- spend time building rapport with you?
- inspire confidence that they could assist you?
- understand your role and industry?
- seem committed to your development?
- employ a balance of challenge and support?
- hold you accountable for your actions?

Coachee qualities

Did the coachee...

- actively choose to participate?
- prepare for each session?
- collaborate in the agenda setting?
- try out new strategies and approaches?
- engage their line manager in the coaching process?

Organizational factors

Did the organization...

- display a coaching culture?
- provide developmental opportunities?
- facilitate skill transfer?
- integrate coaching into the learning and development framework?
- model a growth mindset?

Summative evaluation questions

Summative evaluation examines traditional elements of coaching and training evaluation, including the individual and team impact of the coaching programme. Areas examined include the knowledge, skills and abilities that the coachee will transfer back to the workplace.

Individual programme impact

Did the leadership coaching...

- enhance your knowledge of leadership?
- bring a new awareness of your strengths?
- generate greater positivity and optimism?
- provide greater flexibility and innovation?
- facilitate the empowerment and development of others?
- promote greater commitment and engagement?

Team programme impact

Did the leadership coaching...

- generate a positive climate in your team?
- clarify the team's vision and purpose?
- promote greater role clarity?

- improve stakeholder management?
- help motivate team members?

Using multi-source feedback in leadership coaching evaluation

MSF really is the gold standard in leadership coaching evaluation. Not only does it overcome the limitations of self-report data, but it also specifically targets those who should be positively impacted by a leadership coaching intervention. This is the equivalent of a Level 3 Kirkpatrick evaluation, which is the closest most programmes will get to demonstrating performance improvement, given that job performance is so difficult to individually quantify in most roles.

Summary and conclusion

This chapter is about effectively delivering a strength-based leadership coaching programme within an organization. It is not sufficient to master the technique of strength-based leadership coaching in order to deliver a successful programme. It is essential that both the individuals and organization are ready for change and that stakeholders have been engaged and appropriately socialized to the model. In addition, the process of raising awareness in the coachee requires the careful administration of multi-rater feedback instruments to ensure reliable and valid data on the coachee is collected. The individual preparation of the coachee makes a significant difference to the effectiveness of the programme and this in turn is a function of the internal support they are experiencing. Coach variables are also crucial in ensuring a successful programme. Coaches need to be well trained in the strength-based methodology and capable of remaining aligned to that approach throughout the programme. They need to manage the coaching process effectively, bringing a balance of challenge and support to the coaching engagement. Finally, the gains made in coaching need to be effectively transferred to the workplace and evaluated so that the return on investment is apparent to the organization.

Some questions to consider

- Is your organization ready for a leadership coaching programme? How do you know?

- How would you socialize the client to a strength-based approach?

- Who are the key stakeholders in this coaching engagement?

- What are the necessary elements of an effective coaching process?

- How might a formative evaluation improve the coaching process?

References

Atkins, P W B and Wood, R (2002) Self-versus others' ratings as predictors of assessment center ratings: validation evidence for 360-degree feedback programs, *Personnel Psychology*, 55 (4), pp 871–904

Avolio, B J (ed) (2010) *Full Range Leadership Development*, SAGE Publications, Thousand Oaks, CA

Avolio, B J and Hannah, S T (2008) Developmental readiness: accelerating leader development, *Consulting Psychology Journal: Practice and Research*, 60 (4), pp 331–47

Baldwin, T T and Ford, J K (1988) Transfer of training: a review and directions for future research, *Personnel Psychology*, 41 (1), pp 63–105

Blakey, J and Day, I (2012) *Challenging Coaching: Going beyond traditional coaching to face the FACTS*, Nicholas Brealey Publishing, London

Dunning, D *et al* (2003) Why people fail to recognize their own incompetence, *Current Directions in Psychological Science*, 12 (3), pp 83–87

Ely, K et al (2010) Evaluating leadership coaching: a review and integrated framework, *The Leadership Quarterly*, 21 (4), pp 585–99

Franklin, J (2005) Change readiness in coaching: potentiating client change, in *Evidence-Based Coaching: Contributions from the behavioral sciences*, eds M Cavanagh, A M Grant, and T Kemp, pp 193–200, Australian Academic Press, Bowen Hills

Hamblin, A C (1974) *Evaluation and Control of Training*, McGraw-Hill, Maidenhead

Hannah, S T and Avolio, B J (2010) Ready or not: how do we accelerate the developmental readiness of leaders? *Journal of Organizational Behavior*, **31** (8), pp 1181–87

Holton, E F (1996) The flawed four-level evaluation model, *Human Resource Development Quarterly*, **7** (1), pp 5–21

Kirkpatrick, D L (1959) Techniques for evaluating training programs, *Journal of American Society of Training Directors*, **13** (3), pp 21–26

Kirkpatrick, D L (1977) Evaluating training programs: evidence vs proof, *Training and Development Journal*, **31** (11), pp 9–12

MacKie, D (2007) Evaluating the effectiveness of executive coaching: Where are we now and where do we need to be?, *Australian Psychologist*, **42** (1), pp 310–18

MacKie, D (2014) The effectiveness of strength-based executive coaching in enhancing full range leadership development: a controlled study, *Consulting Psychology Journal: Practice and Research*, **66** (2), pp 118–37

MacKie, D J (2015a) Evaluating leadership coaching in organisations: a survey of formative and summative outcomes, *International Journal of Mentoring and Coaching*, **13** (2), pp 1–28

MacKie, D (2015b) The effects of coachee readiness and core self-evaluations on leadership coaching outcomes: a controlled trial, *Coaching: An International Journal of Theory, Research and Practice*, **8** (2), pp 120–36

McKenna, D and Davis, S L (2009) Hidden in plain sight: the active ingredients of executive coaching, *Industrial and Organizational Psychology*, **2** (3), pp 244–60

Nowack, K M (2009) Leveraging multirater feedback to facilitate successful behavioral change, *Consulting Psychology Journal: Practice and Research*, **61** (4), 280–97

Nowack, K M and Mashihi, S (2012) Evidence-based answers to 15 questions about leveraging 360-degree feedback, *Consulting Psychology Journal: Practice and Research*, **64** (3), p 157

Prochaska, J O and DiClemente, C C (1983) Stages and processes of self-change of smoking: toward an integrative model of change, *Journal of Consulting and Clinical Psychology*, **51** (3), pp 390–95

Standards Australia (2011) *Standards Australia: Handbook for coaching in organizations HB 332-2011*, Standards Australia, Sydney

Using strength-based approaches as a leader or manager

08

Introduction

Using positive approaches to talent management as a leader or manager in the business offers a variety of effective techniques to help development of your direct reports and peers. However, before applying any of the previously reviewed techniques, it is important to reflect on your own mindset as a leader/manager. Using a strength-based approach as a leader or manager can either be a general commitment to take a strength-based coaching approach wherever possible in your dealing with your direct reports or a specific commitment to modify certain existing practices like performance appraisal, in order that they align better with a strength-orientated approach. Taking a generic strength-based approach involves reflecting on your own mindset and implicit leadership beliefs before building capability in the foundational elements of strength-based coaching.

Generic issues of adopting a strength-based approach as a leader/manager

Theoretical underpinnings

We have already examined the models and theories underlying positive leadership in Chapters 2 and 3, so there is no need to repeat them here. However, when taking a broader strength-based approach as a leader/manager, there are some additional theories to consider. Firstly, raising your awareness about your implicit model of leadership is important as this actually predicts how you will engage your direct reports in contexts like performance appraisal and coaching. Secondly, since much of positive leadership behaviour appears to result in increased PsyCap and positive affect in followers, it's worth examining whether or not this leads to enhanced productivity, the so-called happy–productive worker thesis.

Implicit leadership theory

Implicit models of leadership are important as they have been implicated in the veracity of managers' perceptions of the performance of their reports and beliefs about the malleability of behaviours, ability and personality (Heslin and Vandewalle, 2008). Growth or incremental mindsets are those conducive to development, as they assume an inherent capacity in self and others for developing and enhancing abilities (Dweck, 2006). In contrast, fixed managerial mindsets assume abilities are relatively stable over time and do not support investment in developing the capability of others (Heslin and Vandewalle, 2008). The concept of developmental readiness as a precursor to successful positive leadership development has emerged from this focus on the leader's underlying assumptions of the malleability of leadership competence (Avolio and Hannah, 2008).

Implicit talent theories are also important in determining how strength-based approaches are integrated into the broader managerial repertoire. Beliefs that talent is rare and fixed are not conducive to taking a strength-based approach as a leader/manager. Underlying talent philosophies matter as they direct our attention and form our judgements as to who can and should be developed and how (Myers and van Woerkom, 2014). Strength-based approaches are most compatible with a model that emphasizes the ubiquity, developability and functionality of strengths.

The happy–productive worker thesis

The links between mood state, especially happiness and performance at work, have long been the subject of speculation and research. Similar to the strengths research discussed in Chapter 5, happiness has been investigated as both a state (ie do fluctuations in happiness impact on performance criteria?) and as a trait (ie do happier people generally perform better at work?). The research is challenged by some conceptual disagreements about the meaning of happiness and many researchers prefer the term subjective well-being (SWB) instead (Zelenski, Murphy and Jenkins, 2008). A study of 75 directors using self-assessment measures of positive affect and productivity found significant correlations between positive affect and job satisfaction (0.27) and an even more significant correlation between positive affect and productivity (0.36) (Zelenski, Murphy and Jenkins, 2008). However, it has to be stressed, these are self-assessment measures and the critical test would come from more objective measures of performance. There is some evidence that positive mood states can promote greater creative and original thinking, although a thorough review of multiple studies found a mean correlation of $r = 0.25$, which is not especially high (Lyubomirsky, King and Diener, 2005).

Broaden-and-build thesis

This model was developed to examine the impact of positive emotion on a variety of outcomes including performance (Fredrickson, 2001). Essentially, it's an extension of the happy–productive working thesis and offers a mechanism as to how positive affect can lead to enhanced performance rather than just noting there is a correlation. A key addition that the broaden-and-build thesis provides is the link between positive emotion and its subsequent impact on behaviour – what are known as thought–action repertoires. Thus, interest can catalyse an urge to explore a topic further, which in turn broadens the individual's experience of the topic concerned. This broadening experience is then hypothesized to build additional psychological and intellectual resources which result in a positive spiral of increased curiosity and positive activity.

Taking a strength-based coaching approach to your direct reports

Using a strength-based coaching approach as a management style has a lot of attractions. This is especially so when it is one of the skills in the manager's repertoire and is flexibly employed rather than done so in a reflexive and decontextualized manner. So when is it appropriate to employ a coaching approach with reports and employees? The situation leadership model (Hersey and Blanchard, 1977) offers a simple heuristic to help clarify this. It suggests rating employees on both ability and motivation and introduces the notion of managerial flexibility that is titrated to the needs of the employee rather than an expression of the preference of the manager. Where capability or knowledge is low, a facilitative or coaching approach is unlikely to prove successful due to the lack of options the individual can generate for change. A more directive or mentoring style here would be more appropriate. However, if capability in the employee is high, a coaching approach will be much more motivational and empowering for the employee when they generate and own their own options for change. It's important also to remember how aligned a coaching approach is with being a transformational leader (see Chapter 3). One of the five key elements of transformational leadership is individualized consideration which has, at its core, coaching individuals according to their specific needs and recognizing their strengths.

What factors determine how strength-based approaches are utilized in organizations?

One of the factors that determines how positive approaches are utilized in organizations is how the organizations think about leadership (Riddle and Pothier, 2011). Organizations that think about leadership in largely individual terms can see coaching as a dominion of a privileged few, whereas organizations that take a more systemic view of leadership see coaching as a core element of a positive organizational culture and even a driver of business strategy.

Organizations that emphasize a high level of coaching capability in their leaders and managers tend to have a more collective and systemic leadership mindset, as they seek to take advantage of the capability of all their employees rather than just those in formal leadership positions. This is also critically linked to the underlying philosophy of talent managements discussed in Chapter 1. Strength-based approaches fit well into distributed and systemic models of leadership, as they assume that every employee has strengths that can be more effectively developed and aligned for the good of the business and of the employee.

This approach gives rise to different levels of coaching within organizations from ad hoc coaching engagements usually delivered by external providers to an internal and embedded driver of business strategy. As organizations transition through these different phases, the focus of coaching changes too, often from remedial and deficit foci to supporting key transitions, leveraging strengths in existing high-performers and facilitating a more positive and constructive workplace culture. Gradually this shift also requires the enhancement of internal coaching capability, often via the training of specific internal coaches and the training of managers and leaders to include coaching as a key leadership capability.

Beyond the manager or leader as coach model is the development of a coaching culture. This is where a strength-based approach would be embedded in all aspects of the organization from the leadership team down. Factors that appear to predict the success of a positive coaching culture include beliefs in the capacity of employees to solve their own issues, a recognition that intrinsic motivation is more sustaining than extrinsic, a senior leadership team that models a positive strength-based approach in their leadership style, a supportive organizational context where positive principles are embedded in HR practices, and sufficient resources to support the culture.

Developing competence as a strength-based leader/manager

One of the quickest ways to establish capability in this area is to put yourself through an individual or group strength-based coaching process. In addition to formal training or experience in this area, on-going mentoring from an acknowledged expert is essential to ensure the effective building of capability in this area. It is beyond the scope of this book to provide a detailed list of the necessary coaching capabilities for a leader/manager to acquire in order to effectively integrate a coaching approach into their managerial skill set. It's important also to acknowledge that these skills are different but related to those who want to become a professional coach. However, there are some key foundational domains to consider (Standards Australia, 2011):

- *Foundational micro-skills*: These include active listening, summarizing, and SMART goal setting, giving feedback, showing empathy, reframing and paraphrasing.

- *Conceptual and technical skills*: These include conceptualizing the coaching need within the organizational context, planning the coaching process, and evaluation. This would also include the acquisition of key coaching models like GROW and FACTS. It also helps the manager distinguish strength-based coaching from other forms of learning, like mentoring and facilitation. Links here to other forms of leadership, like situational leadership, are particularly helpful.

- *Self-management and development skills*: These include the capacity of the leader/manager to manage their own emotions effectively, model a positive strength-based process and reflect on their own development. Continued skill development can be facilitated by the establishment of coaching networks, coach champions and mentoring or supervision.

- *Boundary management*: This includes recognizing when coaching is the appropriate managerial strategy and recognizing when other issues may prevent the employee from benefiting from a coaching approach.

Developing the strength-based managerial mindset

We have already seen the importance of growth mindsets and implicit theories of leadership in Chapter 3. This is especially important when developing strength-based capabilities as a leader/manager. However, it's important to apply a positive mindset to the development of employees with an awareness of the state–trait continuum discussed in Chapter 2. This is because a belief that even the most trait-like preferences like extraversion can be dramatically modified may lead to frustration and a sense that the employee is developing learned behaviours rather than strengths. The crucial distinction here is the degree of positivity, capability and engagement the employee expresses around the topic. The concept of 'strength spotting' is an important skill to master at this stage.

Strength spotting has been developed by a number of practitioners (Biswas-Diener, 2007; Linley, 2008) and includes noticing where employees demonstrate:

- changes in voice, including rising inflection and rapid and fluent speech;
- changes in posture and engagement;

- non-verbal cues, including wide eyes, raised eyebrows;
- positive affect, including smiling and laughing;
- increased animation and gestures;
- increased use of positive metaphors;
- areas that employees gravitate towards without obvious external reward;
- achievement of results at a faster pace than normal.

Firstly, this can be done more informally than the administration of a particular strength inventory but still facilitates a discussion and focuses attention around what's working and energizing for the coachee.

Secondly, it is crucial to be aware of your own beliefs as a manager around leadership and talent development. I frequently work with leaders who have very fixed beliefs around the capability of their direct reports and then wonder why they are not progressing. These cues can be subtle but are often apparent in the feedback provided and in where the manager focuses their attention. One of the most common areas of upward feedback in engagement and leadership surveys is that leaders are not providing sufficient coaching to their followers. Equally, a common challenge for the leader/manager is to recognize that strength-based coaching is about asking the right questions, not about having all the answers. This is a major shift for some leaders who have been encouraged to believe that leadership is about individual brilliance, not collective endeavour and empowerment of others.

Thirdly, as a leader/manager, you need to be aware of your own biases when it comes to assessing and developing others. Biases are important and serve a function. They allow us to fast-track decisions and make quick assessments in complex scenarios. However, it's important to understand how that can impact a fair and accurate appraisal and appreciation of your direct report. If you don't think biases apply in leadership, consider why there is a consistent positive correlation between a leader's height and their seniority and pay in an organization (Judge and Cable, 2004). But is looking up to a leader really anything more than an evolutionary proxy for perceived power and dominance?

Common biases found in leaders include:

- *Affinity bias*: When the coachee reminds you of someone you know and like, or indeed displays similar qualities to yourself, that sense of familiarity can cloud good judgement. This is common in leadership teams, where the leader can end up selecting team members who look very similar to themselves and consequently the team can lack diversity.

- *Fundamental attribution error*: This bias refers to the universal tendency to make dispositional rather than situation attributions to the behaviour of others. So a hesitant performance in front of a line manager is because the individual lacks confidence, not because they were put on the spot with insufficient preparation. This is a crucial bias in strength-based coaching, as the focus is already on the strengths of the individual. Situational explorations are the best way to counteract this bias, asking the question 'in what situations are strengths most or least likely to appear?'.

- *The negativity bias:* It's very common in managers I've worked with to automatically focus on the deficits and gaps in performance. In fact, many performance appraisal processes positively encourage this. Culturally, too, it can be awkward to focus on strengths, especially if the link to performance improvement is not apparent. I have witnessed many examples of leaders paying minimal attention to strengths in an appraisal format and followers actively colluding with the negativity bias.

- *The self-referential bias:* One of the most common errors in managers and leaders is the assumption that, because they have been successful in the organization as judged by their current position, the skills and attributes that they think were influential in their success are the only ones that can lead to success in this organization. This is almost the reverse of the fundamental attribution error and represents a positive and self-serving bias. (Again, this is one of the reasons we have to be so careful around the veracity of self-report.)

FIGURE 8.1 CSA high performance coaching model

SOURCE: © CSA Consulting (2007)

Managerial coaching capability review

In my own work developing coaching skills in managers and leaders I use the CSA high performance coaching model (see Figure 8.1) to assess their coaching capability. This model extends the GROW concept to include critical coaching skills of observing and understanding behaviour, delivering feedback and supporting new behaviours. The key areas in the model are:

Inspiring and defining success

How well do you know what really good performance looks like? How much do you stretch and challenge yourself and others to perform? Do you show confidence in their capacity to develop?

Observing performance

How well do you know how your coachees are doing? How do you collect information to make good judgements about their performance? Do you understand the context of their performance? Where do you focus your attention – on their strengths or weaknesses?

Understanding behaviour

How well do you look below the surface of your coachee's performance? How well do you listen to your coachee and find out what is important to help them? How well do you know their strengths and preferences? Do you consider situational as well as dispositional factors?

Delivering motivational feedback

How often do you let others know about the observations and judgements you have made of their performance? How good are you at congratulating and recognizing their success and talents? How constructive are you about their shortcomings? How frequently do you offer positive feedback? How do you flex your own style to meet the needs of the coachee?

Encouraging action and experimentation

How well do you do and say the right things to help your coachee make improvements? How good are you at generating actions to help your coachee experiment with new behaviours? How do you hold your coachee to account for the actions they agree to undertake? How do you help your coachee see the positives when acquiring a new skill?

Evaluating and maintaining progress

How well do you monitor and celebrate success? How well do you help your coachee deal with setbacks and derailment? How do you help your coachee stay focused on their goals in the longer term? How do you help your coachee link their development goals to their overall career ambition? How do you help them celebrate their successes and achievements?

Managers can informally rate themselves on each element of the model to establish where their coaching strengths and development areas are. This then forms the basis of their own development as strength-based leaders/managers.

Frequent objections to implementing a positive coaching approach

In my experience, there are several common objections to implementing a coaching approach as a leader/manager. Some of these are covered in more detail in Chapter 10, but it is worth addressing some of those relevant to adopting a more strength-orientated coaching approach with your followers and direct reports.

- *Insufficient time*: One of the most common objections I hear from leaders and managers to the idea of implementing a strength-based coaching approach with their direct reports is the time factor. There is a concern that this is yet another initiative that will take them away from the core business (usually the task) and add to an already demanding schedule. Like any new managerial activity, success here depends on how well the approach can be integrated into the existing pattern of working. Strength-based coaching is an activity that quickly repays you for the effort expended, as the goal is to rapidly build enhanced capability in your reports. In addition, taking a strength-based approach does not require more conversations with your reports but does refocus the conversations you are already having.

- *Coaching is not my leadership style*: This speaks to the mindset of the leader/manager and the lack of belief in the efficacy of a strength-based coaching approach. You are unlikely to be fully effective as a manager/coach with this mindset, so surface the assumptions that underpin this belief and put yourself in developmental situations that challenge these assumptions. Working with your own qualified leadership coach is a great way to build confidence and awareness of this approach.

- *Familiarity breeds contempt*: This expresses a concern, often drawn from experience, that forming too close relationships at work can lead to a loss of authority and possible exploitation. The question here is whether taking a coaching approach is synonymous with greater personal disclosure. In my experience, it's the leaders that form the most respectful and engaged relationships at work that make the most effective coaches, and this includes the capacity to deliver difficult feedback. The other concern is centred around equating being non-directive with lacking authority. In fact, the opposite is true, as it requires greater confidence and capability in the leader to recognize the value of empowering others.

- *Cost constraints*: We're in a tough economic environment and don't have the resources to invest in this approach. This is an understandable concern, but leadership issues really come to the fore in challenging times and coaching has been shown to deliver a significant ROI, so why wouldn't managerial flexibility and a constructive approach be helpful in such circumstances?

Specific areas that can benefit from a strength-based approach

Strength-based approaches to performance reviews and goal setting

There is a growing literature expressing dissatisfaction with the traditional format of the performance review (DeNisi and Smith, 2014). Performance reviews tend to follow the negativity bias and focus on what's wrong or where the gaps are, rather than what's right or where the strengths and areas of high performance are. In addition, the fact that reviews are usually done on an annual basis can mean there is a long time between periods of (potentially negative) feedback. Of greater concern is that, empirically, performance reviews just don't seem to deliver the performance gains they are designed to produce. Strength-based approaches to performance appraisal offers an alternative to the traditional deficit-orientated approach to annual performance reviews. In an exploratory study with SodaStream (Bouskila-Yam and Kluger, 2011), researchers addressed the negativity surrounding the performance appraisal process by devising a process predicated on the feedforward interview, the reflected best self-activity, broaden-and-build theory, a focus on strengths and positivity ratios and win–win goal setting. An initial qualitative evaluation showed that those who participated in the process reported an increase in levels of empowerment, motivation and performance.

This and other studies (eg Aguinis *et al*, 2012) emphasize the criticality of effective feedback in the performance review process. Not only are managers uncomfortable in giving performance-related feedback, especially when there is a discrepancy between managerial and participant feedback, but there is evidence that, similar to other forms of multi-source feedback, poorly structured and negatively orientated feedback can and does have a negative impact on performance. While a strength-based approach to appraisals has yet to be formally evaluated, there is evidence from many of the sub-components, including strength-based goal setting, that those who employ their strengths in the pursuit of goals, are much more likely to achieve them (Linley *et al*, 2010).

Strength-based career and leadership development discussions

Career and development discussions are a normal part of managerial responsibilities and often include the creation of a development plan. Whereas in leadership coaching, this focuses primarily on those elements designed to enhance leadership effectiveness, in a typical development discussion the remit would be much broader and include business development, client engagement, peer interactions and adherence to company values. Taking a strength-based approach allows the time to explore the values and preferences of the individual and see how they are aligned with their career aspirations. The greater the alignment the greater the engagement, and this is clearly beneficial to both the individual and the organization (Zenger, Folkman and Edinger, 2012). Strength-focused development discussions can occur at any time but are frequently centred around other development activities, including attendance at leadership development programmes, or as part of the regular appraisal process. As well as helping the direct report structure their development plan, the most obvious way a leader can assist in the strength-based development process is to identify job-related opportunities that are aligned with their strengths.

Strength-focused approaches to recruitment/selection

There is little data to date on the effectiveness of a strength-based approach to recruitment and selection. Nonetheless, some organizations, including Aviva and Nestlé, have adopted this practice to selecting employees (MacIndoe, 2007). So what does it involve? Part of the focus is to ensure not only that the prospective candidate is given the opportunity to discuss their strengths and successes but also that the fit between the individual's strengths and the role requirements is a good one (Roarty and Toogood, 2014). Consequently, a strength-focused approach to recruitment involves devising an interview process that focuses on both the strengths of the candidate and the particular strengths required to perform the role successfully. This involves a combination of 'strength spotting' during the interview process itself and the utilization of psychometrics that facilitate the identification of strengths. This is not a substitute for the more traditional approach that relies on interview, personality and ability data (Cook, 2009), but instead an addition that combines peak experiences data, strength-based psychometrics and behavioural observations at interview to supplement the more traditional approaches. It must be emphasized that there is little published research about the predictive validity of strength-based approaches, so at this stage they need to be regarded as practitioner innovations rather than heavily substantiated procedures.

Strength-focused approaches and employee engagement

Strength-based approaches are also connected to employee engagement. Engagement is traditionally conceived to comprise of vigour, dedication and absorption (Shaufeli and Bakker, 2004). Engagement is worth considering as, not only do many companies now measure employee engagement on a regular basis, but there is also evidence it predicts if an employee gives discretionary effort to the company and their intention to stay (Macey *et al*, 2009). A number of factors are implicated in enhancing employee engagement, including immediate leadership, training and development and performance appraisal

(Robinson, Perryman and Hayday, 2004) so it would be consistent with those drivers if a strength-based approach also enhanced engagement. The limited research evidence available does suggest that this is the case. One study looked explicitly at the impact of developing realized and unrealized strengths on self-ratings of employee engagement (Minhas, 2010). The results showed significantly higher levels of engagement after participating in the strengths development process, with the development of unrealized strengths showing the more significant response. This is a potentially additive and beneficial effect of adopting strength-based approaches to developing your reports, given that so many managers now have a requisite staff engagement level attached to their own performance reviews.

Strength-based approaches and motivation

Finally, strength-based approaches also impact on theories of employee motivation. There is a wealth of evidence to suggest that, all other things being equal, an employee who is intrinsically motivated will be more productive and engaged than an employee who is extrinsically motivated (Thomas, 2000). Intrinsic theories of motivation have been reduced to three critical concepts: autonomy – the drive to be self-directed; mastery – the drive to keep improving at something that is important; and purpose – the drive to connect our efforts to self-transcendent goals. Consider how these three concepts line up with a strength-based coaching approach (Pink, 2009). In terms of autonomy, strength-based approaches are based on understanding an individual's strengths and supporting their development in an empowering and non-directive manner. In terms of mastery, strength-based approaches are predicated on the philosophy that strengths are widely distributed and highly developable. In terms of purpose, this is where the context around the development of strengths is critical. One of the most engaging insights a leader can offer their report is to help them see the connection between their individual efforts and the broader strategic goals of the group. The opportunity to focus on your strengths at work is a core predictor of engagement and commitment, which itself predicts performance (Harter, Schmidt and Hayes, 2002).

Summary and conclusion

There are a number of general and specific approaches that the strength-orientated leader/manager can take to apply a strength-based approach to their reports and followers. At a general level, adopting a strengths approach as a manager is an indicator of managerial flexibility and a recognition that greater returns in terms of both building employee capability and enhancing their engagement are to be found in the adoption of a strength-based coaching approach. There is a significant amount of research that supports the effectiveness of the manager as coach approach. As strength-based approaches build momentum, it's not surprising that other elements of the managerial domain, including performance appraisals and recruitment, are being influenced by a strength-based approach. While the direct evidence for the effectiveness of these approaches is still limited, the indirect evidence from supporting techniques employed in leadership coaching, goal setting and psychological capital suggests these techniques will add significant value to the strength-based leader/manager.

Some questions to consider

- What are your strengths as a leader/manager? How do you employ these?

- What's your managerial mindset? Is it compatible with a strength-based approach?

- When would you not use a strength-based coaching approach with your followers?

- How would you assess your strength-based coaching capability? Where should you focus in terms of your own development?

- How could you begin to integrate a strength-based approach into your performance appraisal, selection and development planning processes?

References

Aguinis, H, Gottfredson, R K and Joo, H (2012) Using performance management to win the talent war, *Business Horizons*, 55 (6), pp 609–16

Avolio, B J and Hannah, S T (2008) Developmental readiness: accelerating leader development, *Consulting Psychology Journal: Practice and Research*, 60 (4), pp 331–47

Biswas-Diener, R and Dean B (2007) *Positive Psychology Coaching: Putting the science of happiness to work for your clients,* Wiley, Hoboken, NJ

Bouskila-Yam, O and Kluger, A N (2011) Strength-based performance appraisal and goal setting, *Human Resource Management Review*, 21 (2), pp 137–47

Cook, M (2009) *Personnel Selection: Adding value through people,* John Wiley and Sons, Oxford

DeNisi, A and Smith, C E (2014) Performance appraisal, performance management, and firm-level performance: a review, a proposed model, and new directions for future research, *The Academy of Management Annals*, 8 (1), pp 127–79

Dweck, C S (2006) *Mindset: The new psychology of success*, Random House, New York

Fredrickson, B L (2001) The role of positive emotions in positive psychology: the broaden-and-build theory of positive emotions, *The American Psychologist*, 56 (3), pp 218–26

Harter, J K, Schmidt, F L and Hayes, T L (2002) Business-unit-level relationship between employee satisfaction, employee engagement, and business outcomes: a meta-analysis, *Journal of Applied Psychology*, 87 (2), pp 268–79

Hersey, P and Blanchard, K H (1977) *Management of Organization Behavior: Utilizing human resources*, 3rd edn, Prentice-Hall, Englewood Cliffs, NJ

Heslin, P A and Vandewalle, D (2008) Managers' implicit assumptions about personnel, *Current Directions in Psychological Science*, 17 (3), pp 219–23

Judge, T A and Cable, D M (2004) The effect of physical height on workplace success and income: preliminary test of a theoretical model, *Journal of Applied Psychology*, 89 (3), pp 428–41

Linley, P A (2008) *Average to A+: Realising strengths in yourself and others*, CAPP Press, Coventry

Linley, P A *et al* (2010) Using signature strengths in pursuit of goals: effects on goal progress, need satisfaction, and well-being, and implications for coaching psychologists, *International Coaching Psychology Review*, 5 (1), pp 6–15

Lyubomirsky, S, King, L and Diener, E (2005) The benefits of frequent positive affect: does happiness lead to success?, *Psychological Bulletin*, **131** (6), pp 803–55

Macey, W H *et al* (2009) *Employee Engagement: Tools for analysis, practice, and competitive advantage*, Wiley–Blackwell, Chichester

MacIndoe, G (2007) Something inside, so strong, *Coaching at Work*, **2** (6), pp 24–27

Meyers, M C and van Woerkom, M (2014) The influence of underlying philosophies on talent management: theory, implications for practice, and research agenda, *Journal of World Business*, **49** (2), pp 192–203

Minhas, G (2010) Developing realised and unrealised strengths: Implications for engagement, self-esteem, life satisfaction and well-being, *Assessment and Development Matters*, **2** (1), pp 12–16

Pink, D H (2009) *Drive: The surprising truth about what motivates us*, Penguin, New York

Riddle, D and Pothier N (2011) What clients want: coaching in organizational context, in *Advancing Executive Coaching: Setting the course for successful leadership coaching*, eds G Hernez-Broome and L A Boyce, pp 401–30, Jossey-Bass, San Francisco, CA

Roarty, M and Toogood, K (2014) *The Strengths-Focused Guide to Leadership ePub eBook: Identify your talents and get the most from your team*, Pearson, Harlow

Robinson, D, Perryman, S and Hayday, S (2004) *The Drivers of Employee Engagement*, Institute for Employment Studies

Schaufeli, W B and Bakker, A B (2004) Job demands, job resources, and their relationship with burnout and engagement: a multi-sample study, *Journal of Organizational Behavior*, **25**, pp 293–315

Standards Australia (2011) *Standards Australia: Handbook for coaching in organizations HB 332-2011*, Standards Australia, Sydney

Thomas, K W (2000) *Intrinsic Motivation at Work: Building energy and commitment*, Berrett-Koehler Publishers, San Francisco, CA

Zelenski, J, Murphy, S A and Jenkins, D A (2008) The happy-productive worker thesis revisited, *Journal of Happiness Studies*, **9** (4), pp 521–37

Zenger, J H, Folkman, J R and Edinger, S K (2011) Making yourself indispensable, *Harvard Business Review*, **89** (10), pp 84–92

Using strength-based approaches for team development

09

CHAPTER OVERVIEW

This chapter covers:

- Introduction to strength-based approaches in teams
- Theoretical underpinnings:
  - Team necessary structures
  - Team maturity
  - Team leadership
  - Positive team leadership
- Shared leadership and high performing teams;
- Team strengths: assessments and diagnostics:
  - Team development survey
  - Hawkins' five disciplines questionnaire
  - Positivity ratios
  - MLQ team
- The positivity ratio controversy
- Strength-based team coaching process – putting it together to build an HP team
- Conclusion

Introduction

Many of the techniques and theories discussed in previous chapters are applicable to thinking about members of your team. But what about the team itself? What would a strength-based approach to developing a team look like? Strength-based approaches to leadership are themselves a function of the notion of distributed leadership: that is, leadership is no longer the proviso of the single omniscient leader who sits on top of a formal hierarchy (Day, Gronn and Salas, 2004). Instead, there is recognition that organizational complexity and adaptive problem-solving is far better addressed through a team format where the leader becomes a moderator of the effectiveness of the team rather than its major influence. Consequently, strength-based teams have a major role to play in organizations, and coaching and developing them appropriately becomes of paramount importance. Following the format from previous chapters there are a number of theoretical models that help orientate us to what a strength-based approach to team development could look like. Some of these models have produced assessments and diagnostics that are useful metrics in guiding team development.

Theoretical underpinnings

A recent review of team models (Salas, Cooke and Rosen, 2008) found more than 130 models of teams and team performance. That alone tells us there is a lack of consensus within the field. However, within that complexity there are themes emerging that allow us to narrow down the foci of team models into three critical areas. Firstly, where is the team in its life cycle? How mature is it and what is the next stage of its development? Secondly, what are the critical components of a high performing team? What structures does it need in place to be effective? Finally, how is the team being led? Teams can have great structure but be poorly led, and vice versa, so what are the critical components of leading a team effectively?

A significant amount of research has emerged in these areas because teams matter to organizations. This is partly due to the increasing recognition that significant amounts of organizational decision-making occurs in teams and partly due to the recognition that individual performance is usually mediated through effective teamwork, and consequently positive team qualities like supportive behaviour, performance monitoring and a team orientation become necessary for effective organizational performance (Day, Gronn and Salas, 2004). Positive team development and coaching theory has also progressed and offers three different perspectives on the necessary foundations for effective team development. Firstly, the necessary conditions of high performing teams have been consistently identified (Wageman *et al*, 2008) and these conditions are asserted to be prerequisites of effective team development. Secondly, attempts have been made to classify the stages of development that teams typically move through as they evolve from unstructured groups to high performing teams (Moral, 2009). This is important as newly formed teams may require different types of interventions from well-established high performing ones. Finally, the leadership requirements of high performing teams have been investigated with the recognition that even well-structured and developed teams can fail to perform due to ineffective leadership (Zaccaro, Heinen and Shuffler, 2009).

Necessary structures for high performing teams

The necessary structure of high performing teams has been most clearly articulated by Wageman *et al* (2008). They propose an empirically derived model of team effectiveness that asserts three necessary and three enabling conditions for effective teams. Their work with the US intelligence community (Hackman and Connor, 2004) suggested that the essentials for effective teams were a real team composed of the right people and collectively orientated through a compelling direction. A real team was one where there was a degree of interdependence but roles were sufficiently differentiated and membership stable over time. The right people required the requisite skills and competencies including strengths, as well as aspects of character like integrity and the conceptual ability to make complex judgements about people and situations.

The final essential was the compelling direction – that clearly articulated mission that bound the team together in a common purpose.

The enabling conditions emphasized the importance of having a facilitating structure supported by organizational resources and developed by regular team coaching. In this model the enabling structure focused specifically on how engaging team tasks were, team norms of conduct, and team size as the key pillars of enablement. Team norms will evolve naturally or can be explicitly adopted and include the type of culture individual members wish to work within. However, clearly some norms are more generative than others, eg transparency and integrity, and are therefore more effectively introduced by the team leadership rather than arrived at through a process of emergence. Team norms are relatively easy to establish through observation, and making the impact of those norms explicit is an effective team coaching intervention. The supportive organizational context involves the utilization of information on reward and education as well as material resources that will support the work of the team.

The necessary conditions approach to team effectiveness offers several opportunities for strength-orientated interventions. The selection of team members based on complementary strengths, the development of positive team norms and cultural practices, and the clarification of team purpose and individual contributions to it all offer opportunities for strength-based interventions. The necessary structures approach also offers a psychometric to measure these conditions (Wageman, Hackman and Lehman, 2005). However, this psychometric is designed to be used within intact teams and does not offer the multiple stakeholder perspective of 360-degree feedback.

Team stages and team maturity

Stage models have also been promoted in an attempt to describe and ultimately predict the process of team development from unstructured group to high performing and interdependent team. Tuckman (1965) offered a four-stage model of team development that charted the differing needs of the team from individual (eg how do I fit into this team?) to group (eg how effective is this group likely to be?) to task (eg the planning and execution of key tasks and activities). Tuckman's assertion was that individual and group needs had to be addressed before the team could perform its tasks. Otherwise unresolved issues around needs would continue to emerge and disrupt task completion. Intuitively, this appears less likely to happen if a strength-based approach has been taken to forming the team.

An alternative stage approach has been proposed that focuses on forming, functioning and finishing (Ilgen *et al*, 2005). Forming involves the collective belief within the team that the team is competent enough to perform its tasks. Again, this is much more likely to happen if team members are aware of each others' strengths and see these aligned with the tasks assigned to each individual. Forming also involves the development of strategy and the development of norms and roles within the team. Functioning involves managing the interpersonal relationships within the team. Again, this is more likely to occur with the development of a supportive and challenging team climate where conflicts are resolved by the collective capability of the group. Adapting to changing and complex circumstances also occurs at this stage through the collective capability of the team membership. Teams inevitably finish through task completion, interpersonal tensions or a host of other reasons.

Finally, the stage approach to team development has been incorporated into the literature on transformational leadership (Avolio, 1999). This suggests that teams begin as a group of individuals, then move into a structured group before becoming a team and onto a highly developed team. At each stage the leadership behaviours and requirements are different with early stages being focused at the more transactional level and focused on task, roles, goals and relational conflict. As trust builds and the shared purpose becomes more compelling, so too do the leadership behaviours, becoming more transformational with a concurrent greater focus on performance and satisfaction of the team (Avolio, 2011).

The stage approach has recently received some support from the adult development literature that has suggested adults pass through multiple stages of cognitive development during their lifespan (known as vertical development), with each stage offering a greater degree of complexity and perspective taking (Kegan and Lahey, 2009). However, team maturity models are seen as less stable than individuals as members leave, tasks change and interpersonal relationships are dynamic (Moral, 2009). Despite this fluidity, there is some suggestion that novel teams may benefit from more motivational interventions, whilst more established teams require more consultative and educational inputs (Hackman and Wageman, 2005). How strength-based approaches link to the concept of vertical development will be discussed in Chapter 10.

Combined structural and stage models

The two approaches are not exclusive and indeed have been successfully combined to provide a stage-based necessary conditions model (Hawkins, 2011). According to Hawkins, teams need to firstly articulate their purpose. Who is commissioning this team and what must they deliver? Secondly, once that is clear, the team must then clarify internally the goals, roles and objectives that combined will form a vision for their success. Thirdly, the team needs to attend to its culture and interpersonal dynamics to ensure these support rather than inhibit its purpose. Finally, the team needs to engage and connect with its key stakeholders to get the external verification that they are on track for delivery. Notice how this combined model integrates the necessary conditions of the Hackman model (eg compelling purpose) but structures them in order or stages, so that purpose precedes roles which precede culture. The Hawkins model makes an important distinction between task and process focus within the team and also factors that are internal versus those that are external like stakeholder management. At the core of the model is the notion that high performing teams pay attention to their own development and are always looking for opportunities to enhance their effectiveness.

Team leadership and high performing teams

Given the significant literature on leadership development and team dynamics, it is surprising that relatively little has been written about leadership in teams (Zaccaro, Heinen and Shuffler, 2009). However, much of the leadership literature that focuses on individuals, eg transformational leadership, is still relevant for enhancing team effectiveness but may miss the additional focus on interconnectivity, integration and coherence that a team leadership focus brings (Marks, Zaccaro and Mathieu, 2000). Team leaders and leadership build on the traditional leadership foundations but, in addition, align individual goals and facilitate the shared social identity from which additional synergies emerge. In general, team leadership models see the leader's capability as a moderator of team effectiveness in much the same way that team development interventions do. Of greater significance is the collective team behaviour that encourages teamwork and maximizes the utilization of distributed leadership. The emphasis on leadership, not leaders, really comes to the fore in the team leadership literature due to the recognition that the collective harnessing of individual strengths will provide synergies beyond that offered by any one individual.

Much of the literature on team leadership offers a functional approach to problem-solving that deliberately declines to specify certain leadership behaviours but instead emphasizes the function they should perform, leaving significant room for individual flexibility and adaptation (Hackman and Wageman, 2005). However the key leadership functions, including setting direction, operational management and developing team leadership capacity, clearly overlap significantly with the structural models of team effectiveness (Wageman *et al*, 2008). Team leadership thus provides a template for the interpersonal dynamics most likely to enable the structural and process elements of high performing teams. Team leadership also connects well with the FRLM discussed in Chapter 3. A recent meta-analysis of 231 team-related studies (where all published studies of sufficient quality are combined to enhance the statistical power of the analysis) found that transformational leadership in teams explained twice the variance of transactional leadership (11 per cent vs 6 per cent) in predicting team effectiveness indicating how important leadership style is to the development of a high performing team (Burke *et al*, 2006).

Team process and high performing teams

A classic experiment on the positivity ratios in high performing teams was conducted with 60 senior business units in a large information processing company (Losada and Heaphy, 2004). Teams were divided into high, medium and low performance based on objective outcome criteria including profitability, customer ratings and 360 data. Overall 15 high, 26 medium and 19 low performing teams were rated on the quality of the conversations they had within the team. Specifically, they were rated on whether their commentary was positive or negative, referenced themselves or an external entity and whether the conversational tone was one of inquiry or advocacy. The results were dramatic in terms of the different ways in which high, medium and low performing teams spoke to each other (see Table 9.1). Specifically, high performing teams were balanced in their utilization of advocacy–inquiry and self–other references but were much more positive in their interactions than the medium or low performing teams.

TABLE 9.1 The positivity ratios in teams

	High Performing	Medium Performing	Low Performing
Self–Other	1:1	3:2	30:1
Advocacy–Inquiry	1:1	3:2	20:1
Positive–Negative	5:1	2:1	1:3

SOURCE: Losada and Heaphy, 2004

Shared leadership and high performing teams

A natural corollary of the de-emphasis on the role of the leader has been the rise of more distributed models of leadership, including team leadership. The concept of shared leadership challenges the traditional hierarchical model and instead asserts that higher performing teams are much more flexible in the way they engage their team members and utilize their strengths (Avolio, 2011).

In conclusion, teams can be well structured and supported but, without effective leadership, can go nowhere. Team leadership can also be integrated with stage models to suggest the type of leadership style best associated with each developmental stage (Sosik and Jung, 2011). The transformational leadership model (Avolio, 1999) suggests teams move from the less functional and passive element of leadership, eg laissez-faire, through transactional elements, eg, contingent reward, and finally emerge as a high performing team demonstrating the transformational behaviours including team commitment, enthusiasm and confidence that mediate outstanding performance. A recent review of the six published studies on team coaching suggested that interventions should focus on individual leadership development as well as team design and stage of development (Peters and Carr, 2013). Although positivity has been traditionally analysed at the individual level, there is now a developing interest in applying this approach to teams (West, Patera and Carsten, 2009). These developments offer an additional source of innovation for the team leader or coach to apply to their team development process.

Assessing the strengths of your team

In many ways strengths assessment at the team level is similar to the individual (see Chapter 4). However, as well as individual strengths, teams are assessed at a different level of analysis adding a layer of complexity to the assessment. Again, we find in teams that what you assess depends on how to model high performing teams, and this ultimately impacts on how you choose to develop them. There are a number of personality (eg HPI), character (eg VIA), and strength-based inventories (eg Realise2 and Strengthscope) that offer team reports but these tend to offer aggregated patterns of strengths across the team rather than diagnostics on team structure, process or leadership effectiveness. As such these are dealt with in Chapter 4.

The Team Diagnostic Survey (TDS)

The TDS (Wageman *et al*, 2005) is based on the structural model of team effectiveness outlined earlier in the chapter (Hackman and Wageman, 2005). Both the enabling and supportive domains are measured by 107 survey and scale items. The survey divides team effectiveness into three criteria: the productive output of the team; the social process of the team; and the impact of the team process on the learning and well-being of the team members. Reliabilities for the individual domains ranged from 0.65 to 0.92. In terms of predictive validity, the five factors of the model were found to predict 74 per cent of the variance of team effectiveness. The TDS is designed to be used for intact teams but does not offer the opportunity to compare team members' perceptions with those of other stakeholders.

The five disciplines questionnaire

Peter Hawkins (2011) offers an assessment of the combined structural and stage model developed by the author himself. There are 18 questions in the survey, each one aligned to one of the five domains: commissioning, clarifying, co-creating, connecting and core learning. Raters score the team on a five-point frequency from 'not at all' to 'the team role models this behaviour'. Each item is rated twice according to where the team is now and where the team needs to be in order to be truly high performing.

The MLQ team

The MLQ team (Bass and Avolio, 1997) is derived from the Multifactor Leadership Questionnaire (MLQ), discussed in Chapter 4. It offers a diagnostic of team leadership and taps into the shared model of leadership distributed in the team. It can provide not only a diagnostic of what current leadership behaviours are apparent within the team, but also an indication of where the team is in its developmental journey.

Positivity ratios in teams

There is no current diagnostic that will assess positivity ratios within a team (Losada and Heaphy, 2004). However, the three aspects of the ratios – self–other, advocacy–inquiry, and positive–negative – can be informally scored as part of a process check during team discussions and meetings.

The positivity ratio controversy

A seminal article published in 2005 (Fredrickson and Losada) used a non-linear dynamics model to compute the ratios of key process variables in high performing teams. Team performance, they suggested, could be distinguished by the ratios of positive–negative, self–other and advocacy–inquiry that were observed in teams. Higher performing teams had a much more balanced ratio of advocacy versus inquiry and self versus other commentary and a positively skewed ratio of positive to negative commentary at around 5:1. These ratios were challenged by Brown *et al* (2013) who asserted that 'there was no theoretical or empirical justification for the use of differential equations drawn from fluid dynamics to describe changes in human emotions over time'. Fredrickson (2013) has responded to these challenges by noting that both the quantitative analysis and psychological theory still support the concept of positivity ratios and that positivity, like many other traits and states, has an inverted U relationship with performance (Grant and Schwartz, 2011). Fredrickson's review of the literature concludes convergent evidence for a ratio of around 2.9:1 may be more accurate.

Building a strength-based high performing team

Thinking about positive team assessment

As discussed in this chapter and in Chapter 4, there are a variety of ways to assess both individual and team strengths in a reliable and valid way. However, building that awareness of strengths does not necessarily lead to better utilization within the team structure. Team members need to know the strengths and development areas of their fellow team members and that level of disclosure requires trust and leadership. Trust that this data will be used constructively and leadership from the team leader and organizational culture, that development is encouraged and supported. In addition, it's worth remembering both the strengths and the limitations of the psychometric approach. They are great devices for starting a conversation about effective teamwork but inevitably simplify what are, in reality, very complex issues (Thornton, 2010). Typical options utilized in team coaching approaches are usually focused on personality, leadership style or an aspect of team functioning, including role, structure and dynamics.

Thinking about a positive team structure

The Hackman model gives an excellent format to think critically about the structure of the team from a strengths perspective. Beginning with the three essential components of a high performing team, the first question is, is this a real team? Critical to answering this question is the concept of boundaries. Is it clear who is in the team and what is the degree of interdependency amongst members? If members can perform their roles without input from each other, then what is the incentive to collaborate more effectively? Secondly, are the right people on the team? This question is potentially loaded with assumptions about the developability of the talent within the team, but there are times when it's not possible to wait for people to develop in role in terms of enhancing the performance of the team. Answering this question also requires an in-depth knowledge of the strengths and capabilities of each team member together with clarity on their mindset towards development. Do they support the notion of team development, working with strengths and cascading this down to their own direct reports? Questions from the strength-based recruitment section in Chapter 8 may assist here. Finally, does the team have a compelling direction? This is a component found in a multiplicity of team models due to its foundational nature. Does the direction engage the team members, and is it challenging and purposeful?

In terms of the enabling conditions, the concept of an enabling structure has similarities to the right people condition. The key questions here also relate to purpose, in that the team needs a well-crafted team task, members with a complementary strength base, and clear norms of conduct. Norms of conduct are like the micro-culture the team creates and this is significantly influenced by the leadership. Integrating the positivity ratios into the team cultural norms is a good place to start.

Thinking about positive team leadership

It is important to emphasize here that positive team leadership is not just the accountability of the nominated team leader. This is a shared responsibility amongst the team and one of the collective endeavours for which the group is mutually accountable. Positive team leadership also complements the necessary structures approach outlined above, in that the inspiring others element of transformational leadership is clearly necessary if the articulated direction of the team is to be compelling. A further way to consider leadership behaviour in teams is to reflect on which leadership behaviours augment the task of the team and which augment a positive team process. Again, linking these demands to transformational leadership, the team task will be facilitated by the encouragement of innovation around task completion, as well as a transactional focus on goal setting and accountability, whereas the team process will be supported by the individualized consideration of specific strengths and how they can be aligned and developed to maximize effectiveness.

A recent meta-analysis of 231 studies that had investigated the link between leadership and team performance suggested that both task- and people-focused leadership behaviours explained a significant amount of the variance in team performance outcomes (Burke *et al*, 2006). Specifically, task-focused leadership explained 11 per cent of team effectiveness and 4 per cent of team productivity, whereas people-focused leadership explained 13 per cent of effectiveness and 8 per cent of productivity. Person-orientated leadership also predicted 31 per cent of team learning, whereas task-focused leadership was not predictive on team learning. Task-focused leadership included elements of transactional leadership, initiating structures that focused on the attainment of objectives and boundary spanning where the leader scans the external environment for additional resources. Person-focused leadership includes elements of transformational leadership including individual consideration, empowering followers through delegation and coaching, and positive motivation. Of the sub-themes underneath the person-centred approach, empowerment was the most predictive, explaining 22 per cent of perceived team effectiveness and 10 per cent of team productivity. Given that empowerment is a significant function of coaching, this is yet more converging evidence of the effectiveness of a coaching approach within teams. Thus, people-orientated leadership behaviours, including transformational leadership, explained around double the variance when predicting team productivity. Remember these percentages would translate into a highly significant ROI and are only averages that can be significantly increased with a strength-based coaching approach.

Thinking about team stage and maturity

Team stage and maturity is a more challenging concept to manipulate in the pursuit of a high performing team. Stage models essentially try to chart the typical development of a team from unstructured group through to high performing team. Moral (2009) has summarized these stages into six levels of team maturity. These levels overlap to some degree with some of the necessary conditions of a high performing team, but do suggest that teams at different stages require different types of coaching interventions. For example, teams in the early stages of forming have the objective of cohesively working together, whereas more mature teams that are already performing may need to focus on fine-tuning their structure, culture and alignment. Another option here is to perform a quick diagnostic of the visible leadership behaviours within the team. If the team is demonstrating largely transactional behaviours and is focused on task and relational issues it may be in its early stages of forming. If, however, transformational behaviours are the norm the team should be more advanced in terms of its own development (Avolio, 2011).

Thinking about positive team process

Team process is embedded in how team members engage each other and the task in hand. It is easy to intuit but sometimes hard to describe or quantify. The Losada ratios provide a useful benchmark of a positive team process, despite the controversy in positivity ratios described in the box on page 168. Independent of these ratios there is significant and converging evidence that a positive team climate significantly contributes to a number of desirable team outcomes including performance, productivity, and development.

Conclusion

The increasingly complex, unstable and uncertain environment that organizations operate in suggests that teams, and not just the individuals within them, will be the necessary resource to meet these challenges. The movement from leaders to leadership supports a more shared and distributed model that can leverage the strengths of the individual team members in a more aligned and synergistic manner. Fast tracking team development and integrating models of positive leadership and team development therefore become priorities in enhancing team performance and productivity. This chapter has offered four perspectives on how to fast-track the strength-based development of your team. Firstly, getting the necessary conditions right for high performance followed by developing team or shared leadership are both necessary elements of a high performing team. In addition, diagnosing the stage of your team's development and ensuring the team process is positive and supportive will allow a much more targeted and relevant team development intervention to further increase the team's capacity to perform over time.

Some questions to consider

- What are the three necessary conditions of a high performing team? How does your team compare?
- How distributed is leadership within your team? Is it really shared amongst all team members?
- How can transformational leadership be used to diagnose the maturity or stage of your team? What behaviours would you expect to see in a high performing team?
- What strength-based assessments would be useful in a team context?

References

Avolio, B J (1999) *Full Leadership Development: Building the vital forces in organizations*, SAGE Publications, Inc., Thousand Oaks, CA
Avolio, B J (ed) (2011) *Full Range Leadership Development*, 2nd edn, SAGE Publications, Thousand Oaks, CA
Bass, B M and Avolio, B J (1997) *Full Range Leadership Development: Manual for the multifactor leadership questionnaire,* Mind Garden Inc, Palo Alto, CA

Brown, N J L, Sokal, A D and Friedman, H L (2013) The complex dynamics of wishful thinking the critical positivity ratio, *American Psychologist*, **68** (9), pp 801–13

Burke, C S *et al* (2006) What type of leadership behaviors are functional in teams? a meta-analysis, *The Leadership Quarterly*, **17** (3), pp 288–307

Day, D V, Gronn, P and Salas, E (2004) Leadership capacity in teams, *The Leadership Quarterly*, **15** (6), pp 857–80

Fredrickson, B L and Losada, M F (2005) Positive affect and the complex dynamics of human flourishing, *American Psychologist*, **60** (7), pp 678–86

Fredrickson, B L (2013) Updated thinking on positivity ratios, *The American Psychologist*, **68** (9), pp 814–22

Grant, A M and Schwartz, B (2011) Too much of a good thing: the challenge and opportunity of the inverted U, *Perspectives on Psychological Science*, **6** (1), pp 61–76

Hackman, J R and O'Connor, M (2004) What Makes for a Great Analytic Team? Individual vs. team approaches to intelligence analysis, *Intelligence Science Board, Office of the Director of Central Intelligence*, Washington, DC

Hackman, J R and Wageman, R (2005) A theory of team coaching, *Academy of Management Review*, **30** (2), pp 269–87

Hawkins, P (2011) *Leadership Team Coaching: Developing collective transformational leadership*, Kogan Page, London

Ilgen, D R *et al* (2005) Teams in organizations: from input-process-output models to IMOI models, *Annual Review of Psychology*, **56**, pp 517–43

Kegan, R and Lahey, L L (2009) *Immunity to Change: How to overcome it and unlock potential in yourself and your organization*, Harvard Business Press, Boston, MA

Losada, M and Heaphy, E (2004) The role of positivity and connectivity in the performance of business teams a nonlinear dynamics model, *American Behavioral Scientist*, **47** (6), pp 740–65

Marks, M A, Zaccaro, S J and Mathieu, J E (2000) Performance implications of leader briefings and team-interaction training for team adaptation to novel environments, *Journal of Applied Psychology*, **85** (6), pp 971–86

Moral, M (2009) Executive team coaching in multinational companies, in *The Routledge Companion to International Business Coaching*, eds M Moral and G Abbott, pp 256–68, Routledge, London

Peters, J and Carr, C (2013) Team effectiveness and team coaching literature review, *Coaching: An International Journal of Theory, Research and Practice*, **6** (2), pp 116–36

Salas, E, Cooke, N J and Rosen, M A (2008) On teams, teamwork, and team performance: discoveries and developments, *Human Factors*, **50** (3), pp 540–47

Sosik, J J and Jung, D D (2011) *Full Range Leadership Development: Pathways for people, profit and planet,* Taylor and Francis, New York

Thornton, C (2010) *Group and Team Coaching: The essential guide,* Routledge, New York

Tuckman, B W (1965) Developmental sequence in small groups, *Psychological Bulletin,* **63** (6), pp 384–99

Wageman, R, Hackman, J R and Lehman, E (2005) Team diagnostic survey: development of an instrument, *Journal of Applied Behavioral Science,* **41** (4), pp 373–98

Wageman, R *et al* (2008) *Senior Leadership Teams: What it takes to make them great,* Harvard Business School Press, Boston, MA

West, B J, Patera, J L and Carsten, M K (2009) Team level positivity: investigating positive psychological capacities and team level outcomes, *Journal of Organizational Behavior,* **30** (2), pp 249–67

Zaccaro, S J, Heinen, B, and Shuffler, M (2009) Team leadership and team effectiveness, in *Team Effectiveness in Complex Organizations: Cross-disciplinary perspectives and approaches,* eds E Salas, G F Goodwin and C S Burke, pp 83–111, Routledge, New York

The context and limits of strength-based leadership coaching

Introduction

The preceding chapters have hopefully conveyed my evidential belief that strength-based approaches can add significantly to positive leadership development when conducted in the right context with the right methodology. Context is key here, as leadership is not developed in a vacuum, nor are strengths assessed in isolation. So what is the necessary context for a strength-based approach, and how does it integrate with existing models of leadership?

Context of a strength-based approach

There are several key contextual factors to consider when implementing a strength-based approach to leadership coaching in organizations. Consider the following factors:

- Situational awareness – this involves essentially guarding against the fundamental attribution error and making sure that sufficient attention is paid to the situational elements of any strength or behaviour. It also challenges a trait-based view of strengths and suggests a focus on more state-like constructs.

- Relativity of strengths – this is an extension of the situational awareness focus and reminds us that strengths are not fixed entities but more like fluid potentials that are moderated by their context. A key moderator is utilization with strengths over- or underdone no longer qualifying as strengths. Equally, strengths applied in the wrong context, eg being consultative in a context that requires rapid decision-making.

- Criticality of holistic development – this involves considering both the strengths and weaknesses of the leader rather than the partial focus on the positive. It advocates a rounded perspective that accepts the totality of the leader's capability and the necessity of eliminating weaknesses and addressing fatal flaws.

- Integration with other models – this involves accepting that strength-based approaches do not occur in isolation and instead are integrated into multiple models of leadership.

Strength-based approaches are more model and methodology than a theory but are supported and entirely compatible with several theories of positive leadership, including transformational, authentic and servant leadership.

- Strength-based development – this is directly linked to the evidence base. There should be a clear evidence-based rationale for any strength-based intervention. Knowing the literature and adapting your intervention to apply and test the model is part of developing strength-based approaches.

- Transparency of the development process – this addresses one of the key pillars of positive leadership, namely that there is a transparent and positive benefit for the follower in engaging in this process.

Horizontal versus vertical leadership development

It is hypothesized that leaders can develop in both horizontal and vertical domains. Horizontal involves getting incrementally better as a specific skill or ability. So the leader may acquire greater skills in influencing or public speaking but is still recognizably developing within this domain. Vertical development is when the leader moves to another stage of development and gains a broader perspective and new insights into previous leadership behaviour (McCauley *et al*, 2006). The most commonly cited developmental model in leadership is the five-stage model of Kegan (1994). According to Kegan, the level or stage determines what the leader knows (what is object to the leader) and what they are yet to know (what the leader is subject to). Transformational leadership behaviour for example, has been suggested as an output of a higher order of development with leaders expressing a personal value system that engages and motivates their followers (McCauley *et al*, 2006). There is some empirical evidence that leader developmental level predicts leadership effectiveness as rated by others in a multi-source feedback process and that those leaders in higher levels are more effective in certain aspects of leadership including creating a vision, managing performance and leading change (Harris and Kuhnert, 2008). The basic principles of vertical leadership development are outlined in the following box.

The basic principles of vertical development in leadership

1 The constructive–developmental approach assumes that leaders actively construct a sense of self and organization rather than merely perceiving an 'objective' world.

2 The model assumes there are identifiable patterns of meaning known as stages, organizing principles, levelized competencies or levels of development.

3 These levels of development unfold in leadership in predictable ways with each level incorporating and subsuming the previous one.

4 Progress through the different levels involves a concurrent increase in the capacity to process increasingly complex and ambiguous scenarios.

5 Development is driven by the apparent limitations of the current model when faced with complex and contradictory scenarios.

6 The order of development of the leader affects what they are aware of and what they pay attention to.

So do strength-based approaches facilitate vertical development in leaders? I think the answer is almost certainly yes if you consider that vertical development is fundamentally about enhancing the leaders' thinking capacity. Coaching is rarely instructional in style, eg simply adding more skill in a particular area, and most commonly reflective and insight-orientated in helping the leader understand their impact, preferences and strengths. As such it is well aligned with making what the leader is subject to, more objective and therefore modifiable. The concept of leader maturity is yet to really gain traction in HR and talent management circles (Clutterbuck, 2012). Maturity models are similar to the levelized competency approach discussed earlier, in that both assert that different levels in an organization require different capabilities and that these capabilities are scarce and rarely targeted by traditional leadership development practices.

The limits of strength-based leadership coaching

Positive psychology in general has been subjected to some persistent and sustained criticism on research, cultural, political, ethical and practical grounds. Some of these criticisms are now being heard in the domains of positive and strength-based approaches to leadership and its development. These criticisms are important as they help the profession grow and develop, so, in the spirit of an open, transparent and holistic approach, we will engage with them to assess their merit and impact on strength-based approaches.

Attributional criticisms

It is clear that positive psychology promotes a particular brand of individualism that emphasizes individual agency over the collective accountability. In some cases, there is a risk to the individual of taking responsibility for negative situational factors that may be beyond their control. This is a personalized example of the fundamental attribution error that promotes blame on individuals rather than encouraging a situational analysis. An example of this I have heard in organizations is individuals being told they are stressed because of how they think about challenging situations rather than the challenging situations themselves. Of course, individual attributes moderate the experience of organizational stress but this does not justify or excuse the impact of a toxic organizational culture (see box on page 186 on diagnosing a toxic organizational culture).

Simplicity criticisms

Many of the criticisms aimed at positive psychology and positive leadership fall under the category of an oversimplified approach that fails to capture the subtlety of effective positive leadership development. Excessive positivity has come in for criticism as 'Prozac leadership' (Collinson, 2012) where the reluctance to anticipate and prepare for anything other than a positive and successful outcome leaves an organization vulnerable to groupthink and unexpected negative consequences. The often quoted example of the takeover by the Royal Bank of Scotland of ABN AMRO in 2007 is one example of a broader trend in mergers and acquisitions where the failure rate stands at a staggering 70–90 per cent (Christensen *et al*, 2011). So there does seem to be some validity to the concerns around the illusory optimism of excessive positivity. Strength-based approaches by themselves don't necessarily generate this but many models of positive leadership do focus on the benefits and not the costs of positive emotions in leaders and followers.

In addition, strength-based approaches inappropriately applied, can ignore weaknesses. This criticism of the strength-based approach is supported by the fact that many of the current inventories that attempt to assess strengths produce a list of top strengths as an output with no attempt to identify weaknesses. This is a variation of the concern that how and what you assess affects how you develop strengths. Strengths development done according to the model established in Chapter 6 does address but not emphasize weaknesses unless they are fatal flaws. There are also elements of strength-based approaches that assert that the identification of strengths is sufficient for behavioural change. Indeed several strength-based questionnaires appear to advocate this approach. However, there is little evidence that insight alone is sufficient for behavioural change. In fact, the opposite may be true, with strengths identification potentially encouraging a fixed mindset around that domain.

Strengths can be overdone and derail the coachee, and several authors have emphasized the risks of an unregulated strength-based approach (Kaplan and Kaiser, 2008). This is more a risk for the 'identify and use' approach than for those who practise strengths development. Understanding and managing the risks of derailment due to overutilized strengths is a core part of the strengths development approach. The inverted U relationship should be part of any conversation linking strengths to performance.

Strength-based approaches have also been criticized for underestimating the value of negative emotion and experience (Scruton, 2013). Again, this is a misconception of the strength development model. There is no denial of weaknesses or dismissal of the benefits of negative emotions. Understanding the function of all emotions, including negative ones, is clearly a strength in itself and challenging experiences are frequently the crucible from which strengths emerge. Strength-based approaches, expertly applied are more a holistic integration of both, with the emphasis on the positive but without the concomitant denial of the negative.

Potential solutions

Be cautious about the positive to negative ratio in your leadership development. Encourage others to challenge you and your conclusions. Build a team of complementary skills where diversity of thinking is encouraged and welcomed and all potential scenarios are explored. Be mindful of the microclimate you create as a leader as this sets the tone for your followers. Understand and reflect on the difference between functional and excessive positivity. Explore negative emotions in case insights about threat or risk are contained within them, but do so proportionately given our tendency for false alarms.

Research/theoretical criticisms

Strength-based approaches that emphasize a trait-based methodology such as the identification of character strengths are at risk of being labelled as just another trait-based approach to leader development. This criticism is based on the notion of conceptualizing strengths as traits rather than states and focusing more on identification and selection than development. I have argued for a state-based approach in this book due to their developability, but there is no doubt that character strengths bear a strong resemblance to personality traits. Given that traits are seen by definition as stable across time, they don't really make sense as points of coaching intervention. Conceptualizing strengths as states that can be modified fits much better into a leadership coaching context.

Strength-based approaches have also been accused of ignoring the context and system of the coachee. This is an extension of the criticism of trait-based approaches and certainly has some validity, but it is a criticism of all models that emphasize the individual level of analysis. Without sensitivity to context, strengths cease to be defined as such and can become liabilities (Niemiec, 2014). All strength-based approaches, and indeed any coaching engagement, need to be aware of and sensitive to the context of the coachee as discussed in the first part of this chapter.

There is also criticism of some of the positive leadership theories including transformational, authentic and servant that emanate from critical leadership studies (Collinson, 2011). These centre around concerns of the over-attribution of agency within leaders, that denies or minimizes the contributions that followers make and the use of coercive power to encourage conformity and stifle dissent. Authentic leadership is also challenged as the values it embraces are seen to emanate from the leader rather than co-constructed with followers (Tourish, 2013). These are valid concerns but at least partially ameliorated by the concept of distributed or shared leadership that predicate the strength-based approach and mitigate against power and authority residing too disproportionately in any one 'heroic' leader. They are also partially addressed by our definition that requires positive leadership to be self-transcendent in terms of its purpose.

Cultural criticisms

The vast majority of research in positive and coaching psychology has come from the United States and the United Kingdom. This is in part a function of the alignment with Western individualism and leader-focused development. What impact does this have on the generalizability of the research findings and what values are embedded in this approach? It has been suggested that Western and Eastern assumptions regarding positive psychology and leadership are very different with Eastern approaches taking a more collective, fatalistic and existential view that favours social responsibility over individual happiness (Wong, 2011). These differences would be in alignment with more general differences found in cultural orientation (Hofstede, 1991).

Hofstede's landmark study on cultural dimensions converged on six elements, including:

1 Power-distance: how is power distributed within the country or organization?

2 Individualistic–collectivistic: is it the group or the individual that is emphasized?

3 Cooperative–assertive: is the norm one of cooperation with a group focus or competition with an individual focus?

4 Tolerance for risk: how comfortable are people in changing the way they work and dealing with ambiguity?

5 Time orientation: is the focus long-term and future-orientated or short-term, past-, and present-orientated?

6 Indulgence-restraint: is the focus on immediate gratification of basic drives or on self-regulation and temperance?

So will positive leadership be effective in Eastern cultures with their focus on more modest, collective and hierarchical models of leadership? The answer is we just don't know, as the research has yet to be done, but there would appear to be some challenges in terms of the focus on individualism, optimism and self-confidence that predicate much of contemporary positive leadership theories (Fineman, 2006). This is clearly a fruitful area for future research.

Political criticisms

Positive psychology has engendered criticism from those who see the dark side of the positive focus as viewing 'unhappiness as pathology' and potential stigmatizing those who, by preference or disposition, do not wish to engage in the happy worker ideology (Fineman, 2006). The underlying assumptions of positive psychology with the emphasis on individual responsibility for happiness rather than societal explanations have also been questioned (Furedi, 2003). The contrary argument is that happiness and well-being is more mediated by societal than individual factors and that income inequality and relative poverty are key factors in the rise of rates of mental distress and un-happiness (Wilkinson and Pickett, 2011). This tension between indi-vidual and societal attributions of well-being and distress has a long history but has yet to be fully explored in positive psychology. Nonetheless the risk of the abrogation of responsibility for social issues and the inappropriate fostering of those onto individuals is one that those engaged in positive leadership development should be mindful of. I have seen elements of this in organizations where employees are both criticized and held accountable for their low reported levels of engagement whilst concurrently experiencing organ-izationally led drastic reductions in resources, enhanced job insecurity and ever increasing performance targets. The core of this critique, that individual adaptation to iniquitous social situations are aiming at the wrong level of change, is the same as that described in the adaptation to, or rejection of, a toxic organizational culture. Clearly, there are times when it is not adaptive to apply individual techniques of emotional modification to what are clearly organizational and societal dysfunctions (see box below).

Diagnosing a toxic organizational culture

A critical distinction that a leader needs to make is to determine when their negative emotions are functional responses to a toxic and unsupportive culture or an individual attribution that can be modified to enhance their individual well-being and productivity. This list of key characteristics of a toxic organizational culture should help to clarify this distinction. Toxic organizational cultures tend to:

- apply a rigid enforcement of positive emotional expression in the workplace, independent of context;

- apply talent management models predicated on fixed and scarce models of talent that promote the 'rank and yank' mentality, eg Enron;

- excessively apply the fundamental attribution error to leader behaviour, privileging individual accountability over situational factors;

- experience a high degree of burnout, turnover, absenteeism and other indicators of low engagement and mental health;

- ensure that individuals have low autonomy and decision-making latitude with the result that they are unaware how their individual contribution contributes to the overall goals and success of the organization;

- commodify and reduce individuals through language of leadership with terms like 'human capital';

- lack stability, with multiple changes and restructures, revolving door leadership and shifting organizational priorities promoting stress and uncertainty in individuals;

- possess an absence of commitment to staff development with tokenistic or no career or leadership development on offer and no time available to engage in reflection and self-development.

Ethical issues

There is a risk that strength-based approaches can be complicit in the avoidance of difficult conversations (Blakey and Day, 2012). There is no doubt that it can be an easier conversation to discuss strengths, flourishing and engagement than weaknesses, deficits, unethical behaviours and disappointments. This can take the form of colluding with positive illusions in the leader or coachee and endorsing their overestimation of strengths (eg large self–other discrepancies on the multi-rater report). However, strength-based approaches are about titrating strengths, not just emphasizing them, so any signs of overuse are legitimate targets for intervention. Of course, that doesn't mean that the coach doesn't or shouldn't explore the dark side of overuse, low awareness or performance issues. Indeed, there is an ethical obligation for the coach to do so to ensure that the leader is fully aware of their strengths and development areas.

Strength-based approaches have also been criticized as promoting a culture of happiness enforcement where negative emotions are regarded as a form of individual pathology rather than legitimate reactions to stress environments (Tourish, 2013). This is a worrying criticism that emanates from those who are on the receiving end of a more zealous adoption of the principles of positive psychology in the workplace. It is apparent that in some organizations this has fostered an environment that promotes a lopsided position on the expression of emotions in the workplace and that don't appreciate the necessity of a balanced and holistic approach to the development of their leaders and culture.

Separating positive leadership and positive psychology

Positive leadership owes its origins in part to the rise of interest in positive psychology. However, as I argued in Chapter 1, this approach took its time to influence organizations and has significantly evolved into the study of strengths, leadership and positive institutions. I think the points of difference are now important to articulate, as much of the criticism I described in this chapter has been aimed as positive psychology rather than positive leadership and its development. So have the three pillars of positive psychology successfully transferred into the workplace? Positive emotions remain an integral part of many positive leadership theories such as transformational leadership and certainly realistic optimism features in successful goal setting and attainment. However, the positivity ratios must be remembered with converging evidence that critical, challenging and contrarian opinions play a vital role in a balanced and holistic perspective, especially in teams. The second pillar, the focus on character strengths and virtues, has been usefully extended to include states and capabilities that are well distributed and developable in leaders and followers. The partial focus on traits was always handicapped by the relatively fixed nature of traits and their limitations in leadership development (Day *et al*, 2014). The third pillar of positive institutions has been largely integrated into the positive organizational scholarship paradigm which has more of a macro and talent identification focus than positive leadership. Positive leadership is increasingly a subset of positive organizational behaviour with its concomitant focus on states and strengths that are ubiquitous, trainable and environmental in origin. I believe this focus gives positive leadership the best chance of flourishing and developing as a key resource and archetype for the effective development of future leaders.

Practical issues

Strength-based approaches can, if inexpertly applied, encourage a fixed (entity) theory of performance in the coachee. This is important as fixed beliefs about traits or talents discourage the idea that they can be developed, improved and enhanced in both the leaders and their followers. If the leader or practitioner adopts only a strength-identification approach then there is a real risk of the coachee inadvertently adopting the entity theory. This criticism emphasizes the importance of specialist training in strength-based approaches and challenges the assumption that the strength-based approach requires little specialist expertise from the coach. This assumption is based on a superficial understanding of what it takes to identify and develop one's strengths. Unfortunately, this belief in the simplicity of the approach is reinforced by some inventories that imply it's sufficient to read one's top three strengths off a self-report inventory.

Enough about leaders – what about followers?

There is developing interest in the concept of followership as an extension of the decline of heroic leadership and the rise of more distributed and shared models of leadership (Collinson, 2006). Distributed models inevitably break down the leader/follower distinction and make these roles more fluid, but there remain some key characteristics of effective followership. The leader's responsibility is to help create the climate in which followers can express these characteristics.

Key characteristics of effective followership

1 The capability to support and challenge the leader around their decision-making.
2 The flexibility to change role and style according to the needs of the leader and the situation.

3 The capacity to provide upwards feedback that is both challenging and supportive.

4 The capacity to take feedback and direction from the leader.

5 The capacity to drive their own development and shape the relationship with their leader around this.

6 The capacity to educate their leader around their strengths and how to leverage these in the context of the organizational requirements.

Developing followers using a strength-based approach represents an exciting opportunity in PLD, not only because it facilitates the distribution of this approach in organizations, but also because this acts as a counterbalance against potential excessive strength utilization in the leader and the concentration of power in the hands of the anointed few. When this model is adopted collectively as in teams, it's almost impossible for any individual to overleverage strengths due to the moderating influence of the group.

Developing as a strength-based practitioner

Integration with other models

Strength-based approaches are both models and methods of how leadership potential can be more fully leveraged within individuals and teams. They are not stand-alone leadership models but can be seamlessly integrated with positive leadership models like authentic, transformational and servant leadership. The added value of the positive is not yet clear but my own research produced effect sizes of $d = 2.7$, compared to a mean effect size for coaching development programmes of $d = 0.6$ (Theeboom, Beersma and van Vianen, 2014), or leadership development programmes of $d = 0.65$ (Avolio *et al*, 2009), indicating that strength-based approaches can demonstrate much larger changes in leadership behaviour. Remember that when analysing effect sizes with the Cohen's D statistic, anything over 0.8 is considered a large effect so we are talking about some really significant changes achieved with a strength-based leadership coaching approach.

Remaining flexible in assessment

The assessment of strengths is not yet definitive and, given the challenges of its construct and discriminant validity, this situation is unlikely to change any time soon. Current assessment frameworks are often driven by commercial imperatives and lack the necessary peer-reviewed substantiation to provide confidence in the construct in question. However, as discussed in detail in Chapter 4, there are more ways to identify strengths than just through inventories. Peak performance interviews and multi-rater feedback both provide subtle and insightful cues for the identification of strengths and the methodology itself can be transformational, in that it re-focuses the interviewer on what is effective, skilful and capable. This is a case where the strength-based methodology that combines multiple modes of assessment is more reliable and valid than any individual psychometric.

Remaining sensitive to context

The first question for a practitioner is, in what context is the strength being utilized? The organizational context must be fully explored to understand what strengths, in what combination and at what utilization level, will maximize performance. Without succumbing completely to adjectivalism, try adding situational as a prefix to any identified strengths to really bring home the point of the situational specificity of strength utilization. Consider also the interpersonal context that the leader is operating within. Have they had enough diverse opportunities to really know their preferences, and where are they in terms of organizational level?

Remaining sensitive to utilization

Strengths utilization is a core aspect of the strength-based methodology along with alignment, pairing and awareness. Utilization at its core means remaining sensitive to context, understanding how one strength complements another, and how situational factors can moderate the effectiveness of strengths. Practitioners should be vigilant for over- and underutilization and continually encouraging the leader to titrate their strengths against their challenges. Raising awareness of overuse through questioning and clarifying what the behavioural symptoms of excessive application would look like facilitates this process.

Remaining vigilant for hubris

Developing as a strength-based practitioner means refining your capability to have challenging conversations in a strength-based manner. I find the inverted U relationship between strengths and performance a valuable model in explaining how strengths can be overdone and the risks of over-leveraging confidence to the point where arrogance and narcissism infect judgement and performance in the leader. Interrogate the leader as to what this strength overdone would look like and how they can remain vigilant for this.

Separating construct and method

There is a crucial distinction to be made between the strength-based methodology and the construct of strengths. As you can see from Chapter 4, there is still significant debate around the construct of strengths with different models emphasizing states, traits, competencies, skills and personality variables. Much of this variation is driven by marketing rather than research, making the veracity of individual claims difficult to assess. What is unequivocal is that the methodology of strength-based approaches is transformative in its focus on what is effective, positive and flourishing in the leader. This strengths development methodology is most aligned with a state-based approach to strengths, in that these are the most developable and malleable constructs for the leader to focus on. Developing as a strength-based practitioner is more about refining the methodology than refining the construct.

Contributing to the evidence base

The relative recency of strength-based approaches to leadership development offers many opportunities to contribute to the research base. There would be significant value in replicating some of the existing research, as well as conducting comparative investigations on different types of strength-based interventions, to clarify which elements appear to offer the greatest impact in developing positive leadership.

Managing the conceptual ambiguity

The majority of leaders I have worked with look for a degree of certainty and direction when engaging in leadership development. Change and development itself is a demanding and challenging process and it is rarely the time to introduce more uncertainty about the veracity and validity of the leadership models that are guiding their development. However, the practitioner must hold these concepts lightly, maintaining their awareness that within the average profiles of successful leaders lies significant variability and diversity. There are many ways to lead successfully and even the most reliable and valid leadership models only explain part of the variance of this success. So a balance between the necessity of clarity and direction in the leadership development process and the conjectural nature of our theoretical knowledge of leadership must be struck. Positive leadership is not the answer to be held rigidly and applied with an ideological zeal that inhibits further development and modification. However, it is the culmination of significant and empirical and theoretical research which at least partially explains, predicts and develops leadership behaviour whilst remaining open to challenge and refutation. As such, it contains all the hallmarks of a robust scientific model (Chalmers, 2013).

Best practice strength-based leadership development

1 Understand the origins of strength-based approaches. PLD has evolved as a foil to our predisposition to focus on the deficits in performance. It is part of the positive organizational behaviour approach that emphasizes the development of states as the most effective way to enhance leadership capability.

2 Understand the variety of models that attempt to identify and develop strengths. Be clear that how you assess strengths affects how you develop them and that a growth mindset is most compatible with selecting states that are distributed,

flexible and developable. Preference is states over traits in terms of their developability.

3 Reflect on how the various models of positive leadership incorporate the concept of strengths. Transformational and authentic leadership in particular appear to build strengths in followers through the medium of psychological capital. Remember that explicit leadership theories may be at odds with implicit ones so surfacing these is a necessary prerequisite.

4 Use a variety of methods to assess strengths in your coachee. There is convergent evidence that multiple modes of assessment, from psychometric to interview to multi-raters, are cumulative in their capacity to identify strengths. Remember that a positive process is as important as a strength-based assessment inventory.

5 Consider the evidence for strength-based approaches to both leadership and coaching. There are now three meta-analytic studies supporting the efficacy of coaching and multiple studies verifying the effectiveness of leadership development interventions. However, within these studies lies a huge variety of methodological and content variation. Between-subject designs using reliable and valid leadership psychometrics that are based on a multi-rater methodology give the best chance of meaningful results in the leadership development domain.

6 Take a dimensional perspective on strengths and remember their non-linear relationship with performance. Consider the alignment of strengths with business goals, their complementary pairing with other strengths both within and between individuals, and the degree of utilization. Remember that different degrees of utilization, from underutilized to overdone, require different strategies of development.

7 Strength-based approaches require a review of the challenges of the coachee. A partial review of only what works well ignores the growth-edge of development. Reviewing challenges allows the identification of areas to which strengths can be

applied and exposes the limitations of the coachee's current developmental level.

8 Acquire and utilize models of coaching, like FACTS, that embed challenge in their method. This ensures against the process supporting excessive positivity and lopsided leadership. It also embeds the concept of systemic thinking, ensuring against strengths being identified in the absence of context.

9 Evaluate your strength-based coaching. Collect formative and summative data on the impact of your intervention and, wherever possible, sample beyond the level of self-report. Apply Kirkpatrick's model and focus on the behavioural level, especially leadership skills that impact on followers.

10 Consider the criticisms of positive approaches. Can they be applied to strength-based leadership development, and how would you deal with concerns around simplicity, the political and cultural issues, and theoretical limitations? Modify your practice according to the evidence and gather evidence from your practice.

Conclusion

Strength-based approaches to leadership development represent an exciting and innovative development to a perennial problem: how do we develop leaders capable of leading effectively and ethically in contemporary organizations? The strengths of the positive approach are clear. There is a developing evidence base to support the focus on both the methodology and constructs of a strength-based approach. Strength-based approaches integrate seamlessly with existing reliable and valid models of leadership like authentic, transformational and servant leadership.

However, strength-based approaches need to continue to evolve to be fully effective. More research is needed on the individual components that mediate the efficacy of this approach. Practitioners need to be clear about the potential risks of taking an overly simplistic approach to strengths development that can collude with narcissism in the leader and endorse excessive positivity.

Some questions to consider

- How will you develop as a strength-based practitioner?

- Where are the opportunities to contribute to the evidence base?

- What are some of the key criticisms of the positive approach to leadership development and how will you address them?

- How will you balance individual and organizational responsibility for change in your leadership coaching practice?

- How would you apply a strength-based approach to followers?

References

Avolio, B J *et al* (2009) A meta-analytic review of leadership impact research: experimental and quasi-experimental studies, *The Leadership Quarterly*, **20** (5), pp 764–84

Blakey, J and Day, I (2012) *Challenging Coaching: Going beyond traditional coaching to face the FACTS*, Nicholas Brealey Publishing, London

Chalmers, A F (2013) *What Is This Thing Called Science?*, Hackett Publishing, Cambridge, MA

Christensen, C M *et al* (2011) The big idea: the new M&A playbook, *Harvard Business Review*, **89** (3), pp 48–57

Clutterbuck, D (2012) *The Talent Wave: Why succession planning fails and what to do about it*, Kogan Page, London

Collinson, D (2006) Rethinking followership: a post-structuralist analysis of follower identities, *The Leadership Quarterly*, **17** (2), pp 179–89

Collinson, D (2011) Critical leadership studies, *The Sage Handbook of Leadership*, pp 179–92

Collinson, D (2012) Prozac leadership and the limits of positive thinking, *Leadership*, **8** (2), pp 87–107

Day, D V *et al* (2014) Advances in leader and leadership development: a review of 25 years of research and theory, *The Leadership Quarterly*, **25** (1), pp 63–82

Fineman, S (2006) On being positive: concerns and counterpoints, *Academy of Management Review*, **31** (2), pp 270–91

Furedi, F (2003) *Therapy Culture: Cultivating vulnerability in an anxious age*, Routledge, London

Harris, L S and Kuhnert, K W (2008) Looking through the lens of leadership: a constructive developmental approach, *Leadership and Organization Development Journal*, **29** (1), pp 47–67

Hofstede, G (1991) *Cultures and Organizations – Software of the Mind: Intercultural cooperation and its importance for survival*, McGraw-Hill, New York

Kaplan, R E and Kaiser, R B (2008) Toward a positive psychology for leaders, in *Oxford Handbook of Positive Psychology and Work* (2010), eds P A Linley, S Harrington and N Garcea, Oxford University Press

Kegan, R (1994). *In Over our Heads: The mental demands of modern life*, Harvard University Press, Cambridge, MA

McCauley, C D *et al* (2006) The use of constructive-developmental theory to advance the understanding of leadership, *The Leadership Quarterly*, **17** (6), pp 634–53

Niemiec, R M (2014) *Mindfulness and Character Strengths: A practical guide to flourishing*, Hogrefe Verlag, Göttingen

Scruton, R (2013) *The Uses of Pessimism and the Danger of False Hope*, Oxford University Press, New York

Theeboom, T, Beersma, B and van Vianen, A E (2014) Does coaching work? A meta-analysis on the effects of coaching on individual level outcomes in an organizational context, *The Journal of Positive Psychology*, **9** (1), pp 1–18

Tourish, D (2013) *The Dark Side of Transformational Leadership: A critical perspective*, Routledge, Hove

Wilkinson, R G and Pickett, K (2011) *The Spirit Level: Why greater equality makes societies stronger*, Tantor Media, Inc, Old Saybrook, CT

Wong, P T P (2011) Positive psychology 2.0: towards a balanced interactive model of the good life, *Canadian Psychology/Psychologie Canadienne*, **52** (2), pp 69–81

INDEX

Note: The index is filed in alphabetical, word-by-word order. Acronyms are filed as presented and numbers within headings, as spelt out. Headings in *italics* denote a document. Page locators in *italics* denote information contained within a Figure or Table and those as roman numerals denote information within the Preface.

CPSIA information can be obtained
at www.ICGtesting.com
Printed in the USA
BVOW09s2257310118
506931BV00005B/244/P